So You Really Want To Be a Guide

GUIDELINES TO A SUCCESSFUL GUIDING CAREER

DAN CHERRY

So You Really Want To Be a Guide

GUIDELINES TO A SUCCESSFUL GUIDING CAREER

DAN CHERRY

Copyright 1995 by Dan Cherry

Published in the United States of America

ISBN 0-912299-61-4

STONEYDALE PRESS PUBLISHING COMPANY
523 Main Street • Drawer B
Stevensville, Montana 59870
Phone: 406-777-2729

CONTENTS

DEDICATION

To my granddad and dad, who passed along a love for good country and the critters that live there.

Galatians 2:20

ACKNOWLEDGEMENTS

Cover photo by the author. Special thanks to Smoke and Thelma Elser, Wilderness Outfitters, and to Travis Kolbeck and Joe Caliri. Also, special thanks to my wife, Cam, for her patience and encouragement as I've worked on this book.

INTRODUCTION

During my absence one summer as I interned with a hunting magazine, the outfitter for whom I'd been working hired a young man who wanted to become a guide. The kid had completed a home study course for would-be hunting guides, then had gone through a school for "hands-on" training. Within a week of being hired he quit, packed up and went home.

Although the young man had gained a certain amount of head knowledge, he had no real understanding of what it would take for him to succeed as a guide. While no book can replace real-world experience, my purpose here is to show would-be guides what they're actually getting into, then help them decide whether or not to take the plunge.

In order to be truly competent as a guide, any individual must master a vast range of knowledge. Much of it can't be learned from books, but many of the basics can be. That wide array of subjects has already been covered many times in numerous books and magazine articles. Broad-ranging home-study courses are also available.

In addition, packing and hunting techniques vary from one area to another, and from one outfitter to another. Wildlife, vegetation and terrain also differ from region to region. Only a vast encyclopedia could adequately cover all the necessary topics in such a way that a guide, or prospective guide, could use it anywhere in the country. This book makes no attempt to do that.

However, certain fundamentals will always apply to the guide in relation to his employer, the clients, and the profession. Little has been written on the topic. Would-be guides are left wondering what a guide's life is really like, how to best get started, and how to succeed in today's frequently changing guiding profession. That's the niche this book seeks to fill.

A few additional explanations may also be in order before you begin reading. The first has to do with the term "guide" as used in this book.

For the sake of consistency I'll use the word as defined in the laws governing outfitting and guiding in my home state of Montana. That definition seems fairly consistent throughout most western states and provinces.

An outfitter is generally considered to be one who literally "outfits," or supplies, his clients with necessary stock and/or equipment as part of the services he sells. He is the businessman who contracts with the client for agreed-upon services, and thus he is required to take on greater responsibility in the form of licensing requirements, resource-use permits, and liability insurance. An outfitter often guides his clients, but that's only one of the services he normally provides.

In contrast, a guide is not allowed to hire his services out directly to clients. He must be employed by a licensed outfitter and thus is covered by the appropriate permits and insurance. Most states require guides to be licensed, but the licensing standards aren't normally as demanding or expensive for a guide as for an outfitter. He is paid by the outfitter to guide the outfitter's clients, and the only direct compensation he can receive from those clients would be in the form of gratuities.

You will also find that when referring to guides, I most often use the generic "he" for a couple of reasons. First, it saves me the use of inconvenient, cumbersome and unnecessary wording such as he/she, his/hers, etc. Secondly, the guiding profession thus far is made up almost entirely of males, and women rarely seem to aspire to the trade.

That doesn't mean women can't, or don't, become guides. I know of several who are, or have been, good ones. But proportionately, few women do. It seems pointless to be cumbered with the unnecessary use of "she" when "he" is sufficient in the generic sense and most often appropriate in the specific sense. Those who take offense at this may at least be pleased to know I've devoted an entire chapter to women and their unique role in guiding.

Now, before I digress any further from what this book is actually about, I'll let you get on with what you're really interested in. Keep in mind, once again, that this is not intended as a manual on how to be a guide. Rather, it seeks to show prospective guides how to get started, what to expect, and how to survive and thrive in the profession.

Best wishes if you think guiding is a life that's for you.

Dan Cherry

.

PROLOGUE

EXCERPTS FROM A JOURNAL:
A FEW DAYS IN THE LIFE OF A GUIDE

June 1

Back to work. Good to be back. Horses look good, wintered well. Wish the fences had too. Wish I had too, come to think of it. Good to be drawing wages again. Nearly starved this winter.

Lots of work on the fences today. Wires down and posts broken. Forgot how tough horses can be on a fence. Seems like I drove a ton of new posts, and just about that much in staples. Most of it in a light drizzle. Scratches all over from the barbed wire. Forgot how much fun fencing can be. Good to be back, though. Good to be working outside and drawing wages again.

June 10

Spring rains finally quit long enough for Jake to get his hay down and cured. Spent all day bucking bales — again. Wish he'd make 'em a little lighter. Tough getting that many up on the truck all day long, especially in this heat. Twice as bad knowing we'll just have to haul them all back and throw them all off again just so we can stack them again in under the shed. Wish the boss man would have them delivered.

June 13

Done with the hay — at least for this cutting. Stacked up the last load this morning while it was cool. Nothing like a face full of hay chaff to start off the day. Love the way it drifts down and sticks to you everywhere you're soaked with sweat when you toss the bales up onto the stack.

Spent the rest of the day patching mantie tarps and oiling saddles. Forgot just how many straps there were on a Decker pack saddle, and how many confounded Blevins buckles you have to work around —

This is the moment most guides live for, but a new guide will soon find that a lot of hard work and preparation go into the months leading up to the hunt. (Photo courtesy Spence Trogdon/Lazy T4 Outfitters)

especially when you have a dozen saddles to oil and repair. Tomorrow we'll oil the riding saddles.

I'm ready for the mountains. Seems like we'll never get up there.

June 24

Finally got up to the mountains. Just to the trailhead though. Snow won't be off the high passes for at least another week, and water's too high for good floating or fishing. Too high for crossing with horses too, so we won't pack in for a while yet. Just came up with a load of hay, then spent the rest of the day fixing up the corral. Big mess! Corral's still a muddy bog-hole from all the rain, and the feed bunks were all broken down. Had to cut poles and replace several broken rails, too. Tough year on the corral.

June 25

Spent the day cutting and splitting a big load of firewood for the home place. Boss hates making an empty run with the big truck. Drizzled most the day, but had to work in it anyway. Pretty soaked and cold by the time we fired up the truck and headed down. Rain gear seems worthless for this kind of work. Either you get soaked with rain from the outside, or wear rain gear and get soaked with sweat from the inside — plus you tear up your rain gear in the process. Only way to stay dry, or at least comfortable, is wear wool. And I forgot mine.

July 6

Finally packed in for first float trip. Two days in, then pump up the inflatable rafts and spend five days floating out. Rainy again most of the day. Good bunch of guests, for the most part, except for one couple who are both whiners. Even after all the boss man's warnings, they didn't come prepared for rain. Their clothes are wet, but at least we kept their tent and sleeping bags dry. They'll survive. Next year they'll know better — if they come back.

July 8

Jack and I brought the horses out today while the rest of the crew started floating. Wish I could get in on the floating and fishing too. There's some big cutthroats in this stretch of river. But, someone has to get the horses out. Maybe I'll get in on some float trips later this summer. Fishing will be better then — if I can get the dudes to cast a Grey Wulff without thrashing it to death.

Trail real muddy and boggy today after all the rain. Slow going in all this mud, but at least the weather broke good for the floaters. Awful hot on the trail but at least it's not dusty. Took 11 hours to bring the stock out 32 miles. Not bad for time. At least we were bringing them out empty. Still made for a long day by the time we got all the saddles off them and put away, and then threw out hay for them.

July 9

Day off. About time. Can't make it into town, though. Need to get some errands done, but they'll have to wait. Have to stay up here and rest the horses for a day, then make a hay run into the late-season camp. Already time to start packing hay in for hunting season. Rest the horses again after that, then pick up the floaters on the 12th when they reach the take-out point.

Took it easy most of the day. Hauled water for the stock, threw out some hay, wrote a letter to the folks back home, then took a hike up on the mountain above here. Didn't see much game, but some sign. Fool hen acted like her wing was broken to lead me away from her chicks. Saw one marten. Didn't seem spooky at all.

August 15

Ran a load of hay into hunting camp. Long day. Had to go the long way around, since the horses were at the Meadow Creek trailhead. At least we avoided that nasty 6-mile stretch on the other trail. And by the end of a day this long, it doesn't seem to make much difference anyway, whether we took the 29-mile route or the 27-mile route. After that many miles in a day, a few more don't seem to matter.

Hotter than fire, though. Again. Especially along that south slope going up Blackjack Creek. Always hit that during the hottest part of the afternoon. Steep trail, no shade, no water crossings for miles. Tough on horses and packers both. And wouldn't you know it, that's where we'd have trouble with the packs. No trees to tie up to when we needed to adjust Jughead's packs, and naturally that's when the fool horse decides to step off the trail and run one of the bales into a rock overhang. Nearly lost the whole string down over the bank. Knotheads were trying to get at the hay inside the packs while we were stopped. Got to fighting and ended up tangled in each other's lead ropes. Got them straightened out long enough to get out of there as fast as we could. Always glad to get off that stretch of trail.

Hot and real dusty all along the trail. **Real hot.** *Covered with sweat and trail dust by the time we reached camp. Almost too tired to wash it off by the time we had the horses unloaded and unsaddled and turned out to feed. But the cold creek water sure felt good. Always seems to put a little life back in you. Been hot and dry like this for too long. Sure could use a good rain.*

August 29

Heading out from last summer trip. Long day though (or short night last night). Horses could tell we were heading out and wanted a head start. Heard the bells as they headed down trail just at dusk. Luckily, already had Windy and Buck picketed. Saddled up fast and lit out after the herd.

Finally caught up with them down by Canyon Creek, but couldn't get around them with all the timber and deadfall on both sides of the trail. Finally came to an old burn where the trail made a bend around the ridge, and got Buck up through the burn and in front of the bunch.

Stoney was in the lead, and he still got around me, but we managed to get the rest of the bunch turned back. Didn't worry about Stoney. Knew he wouldn't leave the rest of the bunch. (Good thing they're herd-bound.) Just stayed between him and the herd all the way back so he wouldn't try leading them off again. Didn't get back till after midnight. Kept them all tied on the high-line for the night, and fed them grain in the morning.

Second time Stoney's tried that this summer. Guess he'll have to be a picket horse from now on. Got his first lesson tonight when we made camp, & handled it pretty well.

Good trip, overall. Hate to see it end. Really enjoyed most of the guests, and showed them a good time. Lots of good country, and quite a few wild critters. They were really impressed with the mountain goats we saw when we hiked up to Lonesome Peak. Even saw a few ptarmigan up there.

Got good tips from all the guests too, except for George. Has more money than he could ever spend, but hardly tipped at all. Seemed like he was never happy with the service, no matter what we did. Didn't cater to him enough, I guess. Well, can't please them all. At least we'll be rid of him tomorrow.

Getting game on the ground is just the beginning. Taking top-notch care of the meat, antlers and cape is just another of the guide's many duties. Experience is by far the best teacher when it comes to learning all the tricks of the trade.

September 1

Packed in all the hunting camp gear, along with whatever hay we could get in. Made good time. Only nine hours on the trail. Rest the horses and set up camp tomorrow, then head back out the day after. Three or four more hay runs after that, then we'll get in for hunting season. About time. Mornings are pretty frosty these days, and evenings are cooling down too. Makes it feel like hunting season. Butterflies in my stomach already. Can't wait to start hunting. Saw some big bulls in here this summer.

September 23

Rained again all day. Didn't see a thing. Makes for quiet walking, but the critters are all holding tight, waiting out the rain. Just about have to step on them to get a look at them.

Been like this the whole hunt. Sun broke out one day, and that's when the critters seemed to come out. Jed happened to be in the right place when the clouds broke, and spotted a herd of elk coming out at mid-day across the canyon. One big bull sounding off at a couple of satellite bulls out on the fringes. Didn't bugle at him, though. With the whole herd out in the open, no need to draw attention to themselves by sounding off.

This is one of the more tangible rewards of being a guide. You'll also find that life as a guide offers rewards far beyond just getting game.

Just stalked within 250 yards and his hunter dumped him. Nice bull. Dark, heavy horns.

No bugling since then, though, except the one we heard in the middle of the night. Tough way to start the season. Guides are getting frustrated, and the hunters are getting disappointed. That's the breaks, though. Can't control the weather. Keep trying, and maybe the breaks will fall our way like they did for Jed. Just be out there, and maybe we'll be in the right place at the right time. One more shot at it tomorrow. Tomorrow will be the day.

October 1

Tough day. Good & bad. Finally got a hunter up under Grizzly Peak like I've been wanting to, and spotted one of the big bucks I'd seen last summer. Knew they had to be hanging out up there. Mapped out a good stalk and got hunter within 150 yards. Had a good, solid rest over a deadfall, but he flinched and missed the shot. Felt like making him walk back to camp. Had to keep a good attitude, though. It's his hunt. If he

Good country, good hunting, good pack stock, and a good horse under you — heaven on earth for a guide. Throw in the camaraderie of clients and crew and you'll soon realize that guiding is a life in itself, not just a job.

wants to pay that price for a guided hunt and then not learn to shoot ahead-of-time, that's his business. Tried to console him on the way back to camp. Never did get a second look at the buck. Smart buck. One jump and he was out of sight. Knew right where to bed.

At least I did my part. Planned a good stalk and got Clyde within easy range, but it still feels like something's missing. It's just not the same when the hunter blows the shot. Should have remembered to coach him through the shot. He shot fine at the range before the hunt, but they all seem to get excited shooting at game instead of targets.

October 4

Clyde got his buck today. Not as big as the one he missed, but a good, heavy-racked 4x3 with a decent spread. Nearly the same set-up. Spotted it at first light and stalked within 200 yards as it was feeding its way toward a timbered draw. Coached him through the shot this time. Reminded him to relax, squeeze the trigger, and know exactly where his crosshairs are centered when he fires. Made a good shot, and happy with his buck. Not as big as the one he missed, but maybe that's just as well. He'll be back next year for the big one.

October 21

Got a big bull today, right at dusk. Just enough time to take a few pictures, dress the bull out, and open it up enough to cool down overnight. Long walk back to the horses in the dark. Lots of deadfall to climb over. Tough going. I was beat when we reached the horses, so my hunter must have really been shot. Long, cold ride back to camp after that. Didn't get in till 10:00 tonight. Took care of the horses then wolfed down some supper. Need some shut-eye.

October 22

Went to pack in Bob's elk today. He slept in. Figures he'll take a day off and rest in camp.

Tough getting out of all the deadfall on foot last night, and even tougher getting horses through it to the elk today. Spent half the morning just getting there, and spent the rest of the morning getting the critter caped and skinned. Should have at least skinned the legs back last night. Skin was already frozen on the legs. Had to stop and warm my hands over a fire every 15 minutes or so.

Finally got the critter quartered and packed and hit the main trail just after dark. No heart and liver for camp grub, though. Had put them back inside the chest cavity to cool overnight, but a wolverine made off with them. Good thing I got back as soon as I did. Lucky he didn't trash the whole carcass.

Back to camp by 6:30. Grabbed some supper and fed the horses, then had to finish rough-caping the bull. Bob's real tickled with his elk. Kept admiring the horns while I finished caping, and already has the ivories cleaned up and polished. Good color to them. Keeps pulling them out of his pocket and looking them over, and showed them to everyone in camp at least twice.

Got the cape off, the ears turned, the lips spit, and the eyes and nose fleshed down, and the whole thing salted by 11:00. Real tedious work, especially by lantern light. Better than early fall, though. Was up till 1:00 a.m. doing a bull back in September. Had to really flesh it thoroughly in that warm weather. Only got 3 hours sleep that night. At least I'll do a little better tonight. Better hit the sack though. Have to take Bob out after mule deer tomorrow. He'll be easy to please. He's flying high right now.

November 6

Feel like crying right now. Picked up a big track this morning. Good snow. Excellent tracking conditions. Had to be the bull we'd seen over in the Willow Creek drainage. Tracks were heading that direction.

Stayed on it most of the day. Slow moving. Never knew for sure where he'd decide to bed. Found one bed he'd left, but wasn't spooked out of. Just decided to move. Finally topped out and headed down into Willow Creek, but had circled back up the ridge to watch his back trail. Expected him to circle and bed, but not there.

Got a look at him anyway, as he left his bed, and should have had him. Didn't bolt, just stood from his bed about 60 yards up the ridge, and turned and trotted off. Had several seconds — seemed like forever at the time — to get one good shot off. I motioned to my hunter to bring his rifle up and shoot. Couldn't get too frantic, but I felt like yelling. Kept motioning, but the hunter just looked and smiled. Asked him later why he didn't shoot. He said, "Oh, I didn't know that was the one we were tracking."

Still feel like crying over that one. What more can a guide do? Did my part, and my hunter had his chance, but it still leaves you feeling empty.

November 15

Tough hunt. Rained for three days, then turned to snow for the next three days. Haven't seen a single critter, and not even much for tracks. Nothing seems to be moving in this weather. Nothing but precipitation.

Two of the hunters had all they could take, and wanted to go back to camp and pack out today. Had to make a run out for hay anyway, since we're getting low. Took the hunters back to camp, and they talked the boss into sending me out with them and running them on down to town. Ran into Jed and his hunter on the way out. They'd finally jumped a small herd and saw one spike in the bunch, but couldn't get a shot. Hunter said if he'd known the other two were heading out, he'd have gone too. Still snowing hard. On the way down, saw a four-point bull in the headlights, crossing the road after dark. That's the way it goes.

November 16

What a day. Finally broke, cold and clear after all that moisture. Got an early start, and it's a good thing. Only 5 above at the ranch this morning. Got to the trailhead, and everything was frozen. All the gear got soaked in that rain and wet snow, then froze solid last night when the temperature dropped. Mantie ropes were frozen, pack saddles were frozen, pads were frozen, latigos were frozen, sling ropes were frozen. Had to bend the half-breeds around the trees just to get the pack saddles to fit down on the horses.

Went down the line putting a pack pad on each horse, bending the saddles and setting them on, then snugging up the latigos as best I could. By the time I got to the end of the line, the first horse had warmed up the pad and latigo enough that I could start back down the line and tighten them up about where they should have been.

Packing the bales was a different story. Good thing we had them mantied up ahead-of-time. Sling ropes were all iced up, though, and they didn't hang close enough to the horses to thaw from their body heat. Basket-hitched the bales as best I could, but ropes were frozen so stiff they would hardly slide through the D-rings or take a decent knot.

Pretty sorry looking pack job by the time I got all seven horses loaded. Sling ropes still frozen stiff and sticking out all over, but the loads rode pretty well. Only had to adjust two of them. At least that part went okay. Everything took about four times as long as it usually does.

Had to stop and cut four deadfalls out of the trail. No way out around them with the horses. Lot of trees came down under the weight of the snow last night. Got over or around most of them, but the ones I had to cut really set me back on time. Normally would have been into camp by early afternoon. Didn't get in till after dark.

November 24

Pack out tomorrow. Hate to see it all end for the year. Boss let Jack and me stay in and hunt a few days before pulling camp out. Jack dumped a raghorn bull. Not a bad one actually. Only a 4x3, but a good spread to it. This time of year you take what you get and are glad to get it. I hunted down river three days in a row. Figured I might catch the elk migrating, like we did a few years ago. No luck. Finally saw four cows yesterday, but that's it. Should have hunted up high.

November 25

Packed out. Long day, again. Up at 4:30 to start pulling camp. Always takes longer than you'd think. Finally got it all wrapped up and packed up and headed out about 1:30. Good trip out, except crossing Coyote Creek. Creek was frozen over, and the horses were all afraid to test the ice. Fought with them for 15 minutes before I finally got Flame

The satisfaction of a completed hunt, the promise of more to come. Whether you're just packing game back to camp or packing out to civilization, guiding offers good memories to look back on and always something more to look ahead to.

to step out on it and break through. Good thing we'd left him empty. Climbed on his pack saddle and got him to thrash through and break a channel through the ice so the others would follow him across. Good horse. Has his bad points, but I'd take him in my string any day.

Broke out into the open down river and could look back up at the pass and all the snow on the trees. Love days like this. Cold and clear as a bell. One of those days that make you feel like shouting. Wouldn't trade it for the world. Sure hate to see the season end. Could use some rest, but sure enjoy this life. Hope the wages I've saved up will get me through the winter, or that I can find another job to get me through. Not sure yet where I'll bunk for the winter, but I'll worry about that later.

Got down to the trailhead just after dark, but the trucks were all frozen up. Got heat underneath them enough to warm them to where they'd start, but lost a good hour on that. Finally got them loaded up and the tires chained. Roads really icy, especially at the first big bend. Nearly lost the stock truck there. Chain tighteners kept breaking and the chains kept coming loose. Fought with that all the way down. Times like that, you're glad to see the season end, but not really.

Hopefully there'll be enough work to keep me around the ranch another week or two. Better hit the sack for now, though. Need it. Plumb beat.

CHAPTER ONE

SO,
YOU REALLY THINK YOU WANT TO BE A GUIDE

So you really think you want to be a guide. Well, welcome to the crowd. What youngster hasn't been fascinated with the mystique of a backwoodsman or backcountry guide? Who hasn't envied that way of life? Even as adults most outdoorsmen and even non-outdoorsmen wish they could live a guide's life.

There certainly is a mystique attached to the notion of being a guide. It seems to reflect the hardiness, woods wisdom, self-sufficiency and savvy that our North American heritage is built on. Like our folk heroes or even many Hollywood characters, guides seem to represent what many folks would like to see in themselves.

But have you really looked beyond all that glamour and appeal? Do you know what a guide's life is *really* like? One guide school administrator facetiously tells his students during orientation, "All we do is hunt and fish." But what if the fish aren't biting, the hunting is poor, the season isn't open, or you don't have clients to guide? (All of which happen more often than not, or so it seems.)

What about when a client who just laid down a pile of money for your services expects you to produce the goods, and the goods just won't cooperate? Or what about when your employer assigns you a guest who is something less than the perfect hunter or fisherman? (You'll get tired of babysitting him.) And what is a guide's life like when he's not hunting or fishing?

What about the hours of your day that begin long before the client's day does, or the hours after the client's day is over and yours seems like it's only getting started? And what about when you're not guiding anyone, just doing hard, monotonous or tedious work in preparation for the guiding season? Or worse, what about when you're doing that kind of work while the rest of the crew is out guiding clients and having fun?

What about when the hunting and fishing seasons are closed, the mountain passes are all snowed in, the rivers are running too high for backcountry travel, the outfitters don't have enough business to keep you employed, or a long and lean winter looms ahead and you're wondering where your next paycheck will come from (or maybe even your next warm bed or meal)? What is a guide's life beyond the mystique and allure really like?

What's It Really Like To Be A Guide?

What's it like to be a guide? Glad you asked! Here's a sampling of

Is a guide's life as glamorous as most people believe? If you think so, read on to find out what it's really like.

what it's really like. Ask yourself if it's a brand of glamour you would really like to live with.

It should come as no surprise that a guide's day most often begins at daylight, or a lot earlier, and it often ends much later than the average working man would prefer. What's done between those two points in time will rarely be done for yourself. Virtually everything you do as a guide will be done *for* someone else (either your employer or his guests), and despite its "glamour," many folks find it's the kind of work that just doesn't fit their idea of fun.

One guide described his job as several months of hard work for one month of fun during hunting season. (The rest of the year he was unemployed.) Most of what you do during the time leading up to hunting season will be hard physical work — anything from driving fenceposts or corral spikes to bucking hay, stacking hay, or packing hay into camp. Or anything from setting camps up, hauling camp water, cutting and hauling firewood (usually with a cross-cut saw), to such enviable tasks as digging toilet holes for the camp latrine.

When you're not doing strenuous work, you will likely be doing tedious work — fixing fence, patching mantie tarps, cleaning and oiling every leather strap on two dozen Decker saddles, oiling every nook and cranny on two dozen riding saddles, washing and vacuuming vehicles so they look sharp when the guests arrive, or even trimming the grass around the lodge and bunkhouse so the ranch itself will look well kept. (Plenty glamorous, right?)

When the guests arrive, as stated above, everything you do will be for them. From carrying their luggage out of the airport to packing it up and loading it on packstock, to saddling, unsaddling and tending their horses, then setting up and maintaining a comfortable camp — everything you do will be for the guests. Which means you'll have very little time for relaxing and doing what you want to for yourself.

Once camp is set up and stock is tended to, camp water has to be hauled so there is plenty for drinking or washing. Plenty more must be kept on hand for making coffee and meals. Firewood must be cut or broken up and hauled in for cooking and campfires. Then, once your chores are all tended to, guests will want to be entertained with conversation or stories about your glamorous life as a guide.

Most guests will show genuine gratitude for all the work you put into their trips. But others will treat you as if you're a handservant merely performing a service they've paid a big price for. Technically, such people may be right, but those with that attitude not only miss what the trip really has to offer, they also deny you that enjoyment as well. (You'll often find that the more demanding your guided outings are, and the less catering your outfit does, the better quality client you'll deal with.)

Even those guests who have the best of intentions will often have their quirks or ineptitudes. For example, one guide I worked with had the pleasure of helping a lady client retrieve her glasses from the pit of a Forest Service outhouse she had dropped them down. An outfitter recently referred to guiding as high-priced baby-sitting, and you may often feel he was right.

Much of what you do during this time will be in weather that's either hot and dry or else hotter and drier, or else raining like a bottomless sieve. That's during the time you're working up *to* hunting season. Then, when hunting season arrives, the weather will either be hot when it's supposed to be cool, hot when it's supposed to be cold, freezing when it's supposed to be warm, freezing you to the bone when

Many hours and days of preparation must be put in before the actual guiding ever begins. The long hours of hard or tedious work that make up much of a guide's life include such enviable chores as digging latrine pits for the camp toilet.

it's supposed to be freezing you to the bone, or else raining like a bottomless sieve. Whatever the case, it will rarely be what you want at any given time.

On top of all that, you will likely be paid at a monthly rate that works out to a fraction of minimum wage in terms of the hours you actually put in. And unless you are quite careful about saving your paychecks each month (or manage to find a winter job each year), you'll find that your off-season finances will wear awfully thin.

Frequently, guides who do find a steady off-season job never quite get back to the seasonal work of guiding. It is often stated that the true rewards in a guiding career are not always financial. In other words, it pays lousy.

So, are you convinced yet that guiding isn't worth it? Probably not. At least I hope not.

It seems that every time I try to tell people what guiding is really like, I have difficulty convincing them it's not all fun. That's simply

Backcountry horseback hunts require plenty of hay on hand for the stock. Every possible bale must be "mantied" up, packed on horses or mules, hauled many miles by trail into camp, then unmantied and stored under cover. That task alone is sometimes strenuous, often monotonous, and always time-consuming — another aspect of the guide's "glamorous" life.

This shot comes from a mid-summer pack trip. The weather or work conditions you'll deal with as a guide will rarely be what you expect — or want. (Photo courtesy Rob Johnson)

because I've deeply enjoyed being a guide, and I can't help sounding upbeat about what I love. The key is enjoying the responsibilities and challenges of the tasks you're given, enjoying the environment you do them in (Who couldn't?), and enjoying the satisfaction of doing those things for other people so they can relish the experiences you share with them.

What Does It Take To Be A Guide?
Surviving and succeeding as a guide requires more than just the right mental approach to the job (although that's crucial). You have to do more than simply enjoy it in the manner I just described. The simple fact is that many folks really are just not cut out for the job, and that's fine. Not everyone can fill the same niche. Success as a guide requires a diverse combination of qualities and characteristics.

The time was when many hunting guides were just unschooled, out-of-work ranch hands who had been cut loose after fall roundup and not yet hired back on for winter feeding. Or they were out-of-work loggers. They knew the game and the country well enough, because they worked amongst both.

Game was plentiful enough in those days, and the country untravelled and unroaded enough that all a guide often needed to know was how to get his dudes around it long enough to happen into a wandering buck or bull. Beyond that guides were mainly horse packers and wranglers.

That's nowhere near the case anymore. Guiding is a changing profession that, like most aspects of modern life, is becoming more and more specialized all the time. An occasional "good ole' boy" will still make it in now-days' guiding field, but he's generally pretty sharp and savvy underneath that "good ole' boy" veneer.

A successful guide now-days has to be pretty well on the ball. He has to be versatile and up-to-date, and he can't rest much on his laurels. If he spends much time looking back, the modern guiding industry will pass him by and leave him reminiscing in the dust. He must do his best to maintain the guide's traditional heritage but must do it in light of the contemporary restrictions and resources that shape the guiding industry today.

One thing that hasn't changed is that a guide must be ambitious and energetic. He must have stamina. As long-time packer and guide Joe Back wrote, "If you are lazy, stay out of hunting camps; it is hard work and you need all the shut-eye you can get." He was referring to the need for guides to stay out of late-night poker games, but his point was that no matter how well you guard your sleeping time, you'll never get enough of it. A guide needs lots of stamina to keep him going through a season full of long, hard days and short nights.

A second quality all guides must have is common sense. You can't be expected to know all there is to know, especially during your first season or two as a guide. However, you must at least have the common sense to make the most of what you do know, or of what you're able to observe.

Guiding is a learning experience in which each year, or each day, you gain a little more knowledge and savvy. No matter how old or experienced a guide is he must continue to learn. But also, no matter how young or inexperienced a guide is, he must at least have the common sense to piece together what he knows and sees. He must read the people, situations and circumstances he's dealing with in order to make the most of every situation and figure a way out of any jackpot he may end up in. As outfitter Jack Wemple says, "This business is 90 percent common sense."

A guide must also be especially good with people. In fact, to be a guide you just plain must like people. A guiding career is no place for hermit trappers. Not that you have to feel like family with every client you deal with, but keep in mind that guiding is a service done for people — not for the sake of yourself and the way of life you enjoy, or even for mere "paying customers."

Clientele is what makes the guiding industry go. And it's how you deal with the clients that makes guiding worthwhile and keeps that clientele coming back. If you feel you just can't stand people, a guiding career is not for you.

Actually, you will find an enjoyable camaraderie on mountain pack trips, fishing trips, and especially in hunting camps regardless of how

Most any hunting camp needs a big stock of firewood. In designated wilderness areas, where nothing motorized is allowed, that means cutting it all the hard way. Most chores you'll have to do as a guide require ambition and stamina.

reclusive you may actually think you are. You'll deal with people of diverse backgrounds, culture and personalities. But you'll find that the more effort the trip requires and the more common the goals of the people in camp, the more you will enjoy the people you're dealing with, working with, and working for.

The individuals who tend to gravitate toward guiding careers are rarely the kind who would do it because they love people. Just the opposite. Still, most guides come to realize how much they enjoy sharing their knowledge, resources, and experience with other folks who have the same general interests and intents. Not that you won't have some pretty disagreeable clients (or even co-workers) occasionally. But that just means you'll have to dig deeper within yourself to try to help them find the enjoyment they came for.

The qualities and character essential in a guide will be discussed more extensively throughout this book. However, the traits touched on above, as an overview, broadly sum up the type of character a guide

The big stack of hay in the background didn't get there on its own. It represents a lot of hours of hard work and sweat. Again, being a guide requires good physical conditioning as well as a willingness to put in long, hard, sometimes monotonous hours.

Few guides would get into the business simply because they like people. Yet clientele is what keeps the industry going, so a guide must be good at dealing with people. In most cases guides find that the camaraderie with the clients and crew is one of the things they most enjoy about guiding. (Photo courtesy Rob Johnson)

must possess. Or perhaps "savvy" is a more accurate word. A guide must simply savvy the circumstances and environment he's working in, the people he must deal with, and the physical requirements necessary for him to do those things well.

How Can I Become A Guide?

So now you've had a sampling of what a guide's life is really like. You have a rough idea of what it takes to be a guide. Are you still sure you want to try that way of life?

If you've read this far, you probably do. That's because you've realized that it *is* a way of life, not merely a job. It's a way of life that offers rewards and challenges you'll never find in any other job. Which, again, is why I have difficulty convincing people it's not all glamour and fun. It's a life that not everyone is cut out for, but for those who are it's a life they wouldn't trade.

Which brings up the next question (probably the reason you bought this book): How do I get started? Where do I sign up?

There are probably as many different ways to get into guiding as there are people who want to get started. In general, however, there are three basic ways to become a guide, and each one has its own advantages.

Probably the most obvious way to get a guide's job is to simply contact an outfitter you want to work for and ask him to hire you. Unless you have previous guiding experience, or at least experience with livestock and packing, you may likely have to start out working merely for room and board, or at best for a minimal wage. But it will give you a taste of that way of life and let you see if you really want to stay at it.

An outfitter can't afford to pay much for help when he has to show that hired help how to do everything he needs done. And if he's training you, he can't afford to invest much in you if he doesn't know you'll be back to work for him again next year. At that point he doesn't know for sure if you're cut out for the business, much less if you'll stick around until the season runs out.

You won't likely earn much money this way, at least until you've worked for an outfitter a season or two and learned the ropes of the trade the way he wants you to. And when you've done that, you still will likely have only learned one man's way of doing things. But it also won't have cost you a high price for tuition, as would be the case if you choose to go through a guide school.

Going through one of the many schools that have sprung up for training prospective guides is another good way of getting into the profession. It's a way that is working out well for a large number of people each year. A school that is well run and well rounded will pack a lot of concentrated teaching, training and experience into a relatively short period of time. It will give you a broad overview of the outfitting/guiding industry as a whole, the government agencies and policies affecting that industry, and the areas of knowledge and experience necessary to perform as part of that industry.

There are advantages to having this overview before you start into a guiding job. Without it, you will have to learn many things bit by bit and piece by piece, a little at a time over the years. In a job started from scratch with no prior training, this learning process will take place slowly, as various aspects of the industry fall randomly into the realm of your experience. Some of the better schools will cover those areas as part of your training.

Also, having gained an overview of guiding by going through a quality school, you will probably command a better starting wage. You certainly won't start out at the wage of an experienced top hand, but you should be able to start working at a wage well above mere room and board.

An outfitter can afford to pay you better if he doesn't have to spend his time training you in the fundamentals of saddling, packing and caring for his horses, cargoing up his pack loads, maintaining and caring for his gear when it's not in use, setting up his camps, and dealing with his clientele.

Don't take this to mean that you will be an experienced guide after going through four or six weeks of school. At best schools can teach you the fundamentals and give you rudimentary "hands-on" experience. It's only out in real-world situations, either on the job or otherwise, that you will gain the kind of actual experience that produces seasoned guides.

Many outfitters don't trust school-trained guides, and understandably so. Some schools turn out poorly trained students, and even the best

A number of schools offer hands-on experience as well as classroom work to help prepare would-be guides to land jobs and start learning out in the school of hard knocks.

schools can give only limited experience. But well run schools that are in the business of placing successful students find they have many more job openings than they have graduates to fill the requests. Qualified guides are often hard to come by in today's increasingly urbanized world, and a student trained in the fundamentals of the job certainly has a head start.

Remember also that when you get out on the job, you may still have to modify what you've been taught, in order to fit your employer's methods. Although schools may try to give a broad range of instruction, most of what you learn will still come from one outfitter's perspective — and no other outfitter will do everything that same way.

The fact remains, though, that schools do offer the advantage of concentrating a broad range of fundamentals and hands-on training into a short period. Again, this saves potential employers time in training you and saves you learning slowly over time. It leaves you prepared to start out on the job and quickly gain real-world experience by applying the fundamentals you already know. The trade-off is that this training carries a price tag.

Generally, the better and more thorough the school, the higher tuition you'll pay. Assuming you successfully pass through the school, you should start out at a higher wage. You might view that tuition as an investment. But it will take at least several months' gross wages, and probably even a full season's worth, to replace what you invested in your education.

You might come out of school better prepared to start into a guiding job than if you simply hire on at a low wage and learn a little at a time. But you also might put your tuition money down and simply find out you're not as cut out for guiding as you thought or hoped you were. There's no guarantee you'll even graduate.

Some potential students may be better off hiring on somewhere for room and board and learning the ropes at a slower, less concentrated pace. However, don't get the idea that any outfitter can afford to spend much time teaching you slowly and patiently. Any potential guide must be quick on the uptake, regardless of how he chooses to learn the trade. I saw a would-be guide lose his job because he had to jump into the middle of a busy operation and just couldn't pick it up quickly enough.

A third possible way to become a guide is simply to learn the industry on your own and then go into business for yourself. The first outfitter I worked for had gotten into the business this way. He never did guide for anyone else, but was always out hunting, fishing, backpacking or horsepacking on his own. He spent all his vacation time, three-day weekends, and regular days off out in the woods. His friends encouraged him to go into the guiding business so he could spend all his time out doing what he enjoyed. (So all he did after that was hunt and fish, right?)

Actually, this option is far more involved and difficult than it may sound. In fact, in many states it is virtually impossible. Most states won't allow a guide to hire his services out directly. He must be employed by a licensed outfitter. And many or most states now require at least a few years' experience as a licensed guide before you would even be eligible for an outfitter's license.

The man I just mentioned had to become an actual outfitter in order to go into business for himself. That means he had to pass the state outfitter's exam and obtain an outfitter's license. He had to obtain a permit from the U.S. Forest Service and pay campsite fees and day-use fees since he was doing business on National Forest land. He had to carry a substantial amount of liability insurance — for some time Montana has required outfitters to carry a minimum of $300,000 liability insurance in order to hold an outfitter's license — and he also had to supply the camp gear, horses, saddles and packing gear that his clients couldn't be expected to furnish for the backcountry trips he specialized in.

Maybe a good example of the various ways to get into guiding comes from the first outfit I worked for. When I showed up on the scene, I worked with another guide who was in his fourth year with the outfit. He'd had plenty of hunting experience but no real horse or packing experience, so he simply showed up on the outfitter's doorstep and asked to hire on. The outfitter had written a book on a wilderness area, and the would-be guide had read it. He had been impressed, and he told the outfitter he wanted to work for the man who had written the book.

The outfitter was struggling in his small operation and couldn't afford to hire any help, so the two went their separate ways. But not long after, the would-be guide came back again and offered to work merely in exchange for room and board. The outfitter probably couldn't afford even that, but he was so impressed with the young man's determination, desire and persistence that he took him on for the agreed-upon wage. The

By starting with the basics and building from there, a quality school can give you knowledge and experience that might take years to learn on the job. The trade-off is that schooling comes with a price tag.

Once you've become a guide and the game is on the ground, you'll find that that's when the work really starts. Caping, skinning, packing and then the tedious chore of fleshing the cape are frequent tasks of successful guides. (Photos courtesy Wildlife Adventures, Inc.)

guide served him well for the next five years.

Like the guide I just described, I had a good bit of western hunting experience but little experience with horses or mules. I assumed that no outfitter would hire me on that way, so I decided to go through one of the numerous schools for guides, and I chose the one that I thought suited me best. Upon graduating I was placed with an outfitter who badly needed help, and I was given a pretty good wage for a first-year guide.

The outfitter had to put very little time and effort into training me himself, and I was able to work right in and take responsibility quickly within his operation. As a result, I was earning as high a wage in my second year there as the previous guide was in his fourth year. However, because I had gone the school route, I was out a big chunk of money to start with.

I started work in September, which gave me only about three months' work that year. I was well into my second season before my wages had netted back the amount of money I had put into going to school. And I still hadn't replaced the cost of boots, clothing and certain other gear I had needed for my job. The other guide hadn't had any tuition costs or loans to repay.

The outfitter for whom we both worked is the one who went directly into business for himself. He started out guiding hunts on his vacation time, doing all the camp set-up, wood-cutting, wrangling, saddling, guiding, packing, cooking and camp chores himself. When he finally thought he could afford to branch out into business full time, he struggled to keep his small operation afloat, and he often depended on the help of loyal friends.

The outfitter fought tooth-and-nail to make his floundering business succeed, and his wife sacrificed a great deal to help him out. He loved the life-style and challenges his business offered, and eventually he built it up to where his head was above water — but he still struggled continually to keep it there. He often had difficulty finding good help.

My first employer recently sold his outfitting business and has no regrets that he spent twenty years doing what he did to make it go. However, the other guide and I (as well as all the others he employed over the years) had a much easier way of starting out.

There is one other way of becoming a guide. It's probably the most ideal, but it is rarely possible for most folks. I recently met a former guide who, without necessarily trying, caught an outfitter's attention by being a capable and successful hunter. The outfitter noticed the man's ability, and when he needed an extra hand he approached the hunter and said, "You seem to do well. Would you like to guide for me?"

The hunter had come from the Midwest to hunt in that part of Montana for many years. By learning the country, the game it held, and how to hunt them over the years he had proven his ability. When asked to be a guide, he happened to need the extra work and had the time to do it. And the outfitter already knew he was getting help he could count on.

That situation is the best one, both for the outfitter and the guide. The guide already has real-world experience and has demonstrated his ability. The outfitter has seen the guide's capability and knows he can trust him with his clients. Unfortunately, not every would-be guide has the opportunity to gain that experience ahead-of-time. That's why I've written about other ways of getting started.

Each way of becoming a guide has its own advantages as well as certain drawbacks. Only you can decide for yourself if a guide's life is for you, if you have what it takes, and which way of getting started is best for you.

CHAPTER TWO

WHAT IT REALLY TAKES TO BE A GUIDE

Now that you have a rough idea what it's like to be a guide, and basically how to get started, you must think you have what it takes. At least you continued reading, which shows you're still interested.

However, at best the previous chapter gave only a broad overview of the stuff good guides are made of. A more specific look might give you a better idea what you're getting into — and if you're cut out for it.

It would be tough to list all the traits of an ideal guide without overlooking some and overlapping in certain areas. And every outfitter or guide (or client) would come up with a slightly different list. However, based on my own experience working with a number of top-notch guides, the following is a pretty thorough break-down of the qualities you'll need for success.

Positive Attitude

Outfitter and guide-training instructor Jerry Malson recently asked me, "What's the most important tool a guide can bring with him to a job?"

His answer was simple: "A smile!"

And he's right.

As with any aspect of life, your attitude can and will affect everything you do as a guide — in either a positive or negative way. And given that guiding is a life in itself, not merely a job, the attitude with which you approach your duties as a guide will make or break your success.

It has been said that no man is an island unto himself, and that's definitely true of a guide. Everything you do as a guide either affects

Guiding often involves working under unpleasant conditions or circumstances. A smile and a positive attitude are always an asset, if not a requirement, on the job. (Photo courtesy Rob Johnson)

someone else or is affected by someone else — the clients you're dealing with, the crew you're working with, the outfitter you're working for, even the camp cook. Not everything they do or say will please you, and vice versa. But whether little differences will become major problems depends largely on how you approach them.

What's more, everything you do as a guide will be affected by circumstances beyond your control — anything from the weather to trouble with the pack strings to mechanical problems or other equipment breakdowns. And again, whether little problems become monumental depends largely on your attitude. You can take them as extra challenges of the job, or you can let them drag you, and everyone affected by you, down.

Maybe the most striking example that I've seen in this area comes not exactly from a guide, but worse yet, from an outfitter. Although I encountered him only briefly at an outfitters' convention, a one-hour meeting is all I needed to see that he always carried a slight chip on his shoulder. No matter what point was brought up, he always had a slightly negative challenge to some aspect of what was being discussed. I can only imagine what it would have been like to work for (or with) a man like that, or even to be his client.

I know of other situations as well where a dissatisfied guide began to complain, and another quickly joined in. The situation soon snowballed into a much worse state of affairs than if the guides had approached things more positively, or at least kept their negative thoughts to themselves.

However, I've also witnessed plenty of situations where the whole camp enjoyed even the worst circumstances because one of the guides (or even the whole crew) had a smile and a good attitude about everything that came his way. As Malson says, "If the guides are out there having a good time, the clients start having a good time." That's crucial to your success as a guide.

Ambition, or Will-Work-Hard Attitude

This goes hand-in-hand with the attitude I just described, and it's just as essential to everything you will do as a guide. The fact is, in most guiding operations there will be little time for pursuing your own interests. In fact, there will be little time that is not spent working in one form or another, which makes an ambitious, hard-working attitude absolutely essential in a guide.

As I mentioned in the first chapter, your day as a guide will have been long underway by the time the client's begins. If you're on a pack trip or hunting trip, you'll likely have been out catching and loading horses, or wrangling them into camp, then brushing and saddling them, or readying your own gear. After the cook calls the guests and crew to breakfast and you've wolfed down enough to get you through the day, you'll be launching into more get-ready chores while the guests make their own preparation for the day.

After you've spent a good long day packing up and moving camp or guiding hunting or fishing clients, you'll still have camp to re-set, horses to unsaddle and tend, or boats and other gear to take care of. Then after your day's work is done, there still may be dishes to wash, trophies to care for, or guests to entertain around the campfire.

It's not always the strenuous tasks that a guide must tend to. He must be willing and able to be a "jack of all trades," including camp cook and dishwasher, at least in spike camps. (Photo courtesy Wildlife Adventures, Inc.)

An ambitious attitude goes beyond just doing willingly what you're asked or expected to do. A quality guide is always looking to go the extra mile, both for his boss and for the clients. Guests will often want explanations or answers to questions, or instruction on how to better use their gear (or yours), and they will appreciate the extra effort you put into making their trip. And in addition to dealing with clients and doing your normal camp work, there are always woodpiles to keep stocked, lanterns to keep refueled, and water buckets to keep full.

Even when you're at the home base, I have yet to see the ranch that couldn't use a little extra work, whether it's mending fence, repairing gear or even just keeping the lawn in good shape. A guide who is always looking for what little extra he can do, rather than how little he has to do, will be a valuable asset to any operation.

Stamina, Good Physical Conditioning

Stamina is essential in a guiding career. Not so much because it is needed for dealing with most clients, but rather because most any type of guiding requires a season full of long days and short nights. It often involves strenuous work in preparation for the actual guiding season. Continual wear and tear will slowly take its toll, and a lack of physical as well as mental endurance will begin to tell by season's end.

One of the outfitters I've worked for made an important point. By the end of every trip, he said, the guests were worn down and tired, but we couldn't afford to be. We had to be ready for a new batch of hunters or summer guests full of enthusiasm and ready to go.

Many guiding operations start their season with spring bear hunts, when daylight is long and sleep time is short. They continue on with summer pack trips and fishing trips followed by strenuous pack-in and set-up of hunting camps. Finally, when the long, hard days of fall hunting season arrive, stamina becomes absolutely crucial.

Even in the short run, good physical condition is essential. Most of the ranch work and camp set-up in preparation for the meat of the season involves hard physical work. Horse operations must lay in a good supply of hay for their stock; backcountry camps need a big supply of wood cut, split and stacked; corrals usually need repair from one year to the next; fence posts continually need replacing, and the list could go on from there. Much of the general ranch work of most guiding operations is just plain physically demanding in itself.

Dependability

No guide is worth his salt if he can't be counted on. He must be dependable not just when the chips are down, but in all the routine details of his job. An outfitter usually has so many details to oversee that he just can't supervise every function of his operation. He has to be able to count on his guides not only to get a job done, oftentimes alone, but also to get it done well.

You may be turned loose with a string of mules and thousands of dollars worth of gear to pack into hunting camp. Or you may simply be given a minor task such as splitting kindling for the wood stove. Either way your boss needs to know you won't cut him short — either on time or quality.

Taking a guiding job most often means committing for the entire season, no matter what other opportunities or circumstances come along. I once had to turn down a chance at a job with a well known outdoor magazine because the offer came the day before hunting season. I

A guide must be willing to do whatever needs done — even such glamorous tasks as setting up the camp latrine. But he must also be willing to go the extra mile, doing more than just what he's asked or told to do.

couldn't back out on my employer on such short notice.

Good guides, and even not-so-good ones, are usually difficult to find. They're even more difficult to replace in the middle of a hunting or fishing season. An outfitter must plan and book his hunts a good deal of time in advance, and once his help has committed for the season, he can rarely afford to have them back out.

Drinking and plain old laziness are two common reasons for lack of dependability in guides. These problems will be discussed in more detail later, but be aware that they don't mix well with a guiding career. A guide who, for whatever reason, can't be counted on to keep a commitment, to do a job well, and to keep an agreed-upon time schedule barring circumstances beyond his control, is of little value to any outfit. He can look forward to an abbreviated guiding career. Dependability is a character trait essential in any guide.

Common Sense and Resourcefulness

If you want to become a guide, what's most important is not what you know at this point, but what you're able to learn and put to use. And the key ingredient to accomplishing that is simple common sense. A guide is continually in a position of having to make decisions on his own, whether he's packing a load of gear into camp, trying to put a client onto game, or just doing repairs around the home place. He has to have the simple sense to evaluate the circumstances and the resources at hand, then make smart decisions.

Maybe the following story will illustrate my point. Early in my third season as a guide, the rest of the crew was in the backcountry on a summer pack trip while I was given some duties at the ranch and trailhead to tend to. Then, toward the end of that week I was expected to move a load of stock from one trailhead corral to another, and meet the crew there when they came out.

While swerving around a chuckhole, I got a rear dual of the stock truck out onto the shoulder of the road. The shoulder was much softer than I realized, and as it began to give way the truck lurched. Naturally, the horses' weight shifted that way, and I found myself fighting to keep the truck on the road.

With two of the horses being good-sized Belgians, I was fighting a losing battle. The truck went off the road, and the fact that I sideswiped a couple of lodgepole pines that had happened to grow in the right place was all that kept the truck from rolling.

Cutting and splitting a season's supply of firewood is one of many strenuous tasks that go into setting up a quality camp in preparation for the long, hard days of hunting season. Good physical condition and endurance are a must. (Photo courtesy Wildlife Adventures, Inc.)

I managed to get the horses all rearranged the way they belonged, then hauled them on over to the other trailhead. Fortunately, most of them had only minor scrapes or bruises, but one had an inch-wide gash where her upper lip had been split crosswise. She had no trouble calmly munching hay while I unloaded the other stock, and I figured she was probably fine. But since she had been loaned to the outfit, and wasn't actually ours, I decided I better get her to a vet.

If you can imagine the cost of fuel for a full-sized stock truck, you know my employer disliked making an empty run, especially on the 70-mile drive between the ranch and trailhead. But I felt I had to get the injured horse home, then return the truck to the trailhead in case any others needed to come down to the ranch at the end of the pack trip. So after taking the horse to a vet, I tried to make the best of a bad situation.

Hay is always in precious short supply in the mountains, and amidst a busy summer schedule it's difficult getting enough of it to the trailhead. In order to avoid burning gas on an empty run back to the trailhead, I contacted the farmer from which my employer bought hay and arranged to pick up a load. After the dubious pleasure of loading 120 bales on the stock truck, I drove back to face the outfitter as he and the crew and guests came out of the hills.

In the midst of all this, my boss had also been short on horses that season, and I had encountered a man with a relatively good one to sell. Someone else was also looking at the horse, and I hated to let the opportunity slip through my boss' fingers. So unbeknownst to him I made arrangements to put the mare in with our stock so he could pay for her when he came out. I made sure in the agreement that if he showed up and didn't want the mare, he was under no obligation to go through with the purchase.

When the riders got out to the trailhead, my boss was greeted with the sight of a slightly bent rack on his stock truck and one less packhorse than he had expected. However, he was also greeted with an extra load of hay and a much-needed saddle horse. His disappointment at the mishap was somewhat appeased by the fact that I'd been able to make the best of a bad situation. He appreciated the fact that I took some common sense initiative under the circumstances at hand.

Probably the one quality that separates a top-notch guide from one that just gets by is an ability to assess a given situation and make the most of it. A guide needs to be able to read the stock, vehicles, and equipment he deals with. He must be able to read the game and its sign,

Not all outfitters like using pack stock, and not all country is horse country. You may have to pack clients' game out on your back. Are you up to it physically?

The back-tiring job of shoeing horses often falls a guide's way. When a shoe has been thrown or broken, it must often be replaced under less than ideal conditions, making the most of what tools are on hand. Will you still be up to it after a long, tiring day on the trail?

the weather patterns, and the country he's guiding in. And he needs to be able to read the people, both clients and crew, that he deals with. What is important is not always how much he knows about any of these — knowledge will come with time. What's important is whether or not that guide has the common sense needed to understand the situation at hand and make the most of it on the basis of what he does know.

Resourcefulness goes hand-in-hand with common sense. A guide must make the most not only of his circumstances, but also of the materials he has at hand. I know of an old-time packer who was around long before the proliferation of commercial elk calls. He made himself an effective bugle from a hollowed-out goat horn and a clarinet reed. I read of another guide who used a rolled-up topographical map in place of a forgotten grunt tube and managed to call a big bull in for his client.

You can carry only so much in the way of repair kits, emergency provisions, etc. Whether equipment breaks down in the field, some wily critter you're after requires an unusual twist in your hunting tactics, or an injury or some other emergency occurs, a guide must be resourceful enough to make the best of each situation with whatever supplies and smarts he has.

Ability To Communicate

Good communication is fundamental to the success of any outfitting operation. Most of it must be carried out by the outfitter long before his client shows up on the scene. That way the client won't run in to unexpected surprises, and the guide won't be subjected to wrong expectations on the client's part.

However, communication is still vital not only between the guide and the clients, but also between the guide and his co-workers as well as his employer. Assuming that people know what you know or what your intentions are can prove disastrous.

You can never assume that the outfitter knows a piece of equipment is broken, or one of his vehicles isn't working properly, or one of his horses is sick or sored up. He needs to be made aware of any problems before they get worse, so that his stock or equipment won't be out of working order at a time when they're urgently needed. Better to inform him of what he already knows than risk leaving him uninformed.

You can also never assume that a client understands what you're thinking. You must be sure that he clearly comprehends what you are trying to accomplish, and why. And he needs to know what you expect

Even days off (if you get any as a guide) are often spent making unexpected repairs. In the backcountry, with limited tools and material, a guide must learn to be resourceful

of him. For example, a guide can't just assume his client knows just how to place his fly so it will drift naturally into a prime hole, or how to play a big trout he's hooked into. You can't assume your hunter has accurately estimated the range when he draws down on a big buck or bull — or that he knows where he should hold his crosshairs for a particular shot. I once guided a hunter who almost waited too long to get a shot off at a big bull elk. He was waiting for me to tell him to shoot. I assumed he would shoot when he was ready.

If you split up with a hunter and tell him you'll meet him at a certain spot, be sure to give a very clear description of how to get there and exactly how to recognize that spot. Or if you tell a fishing client that you'll move the horses upstream and pick him up at a certain spot, be sure he understands exactly where that point is. There's little worse than getting someone lost — or waiting and wondering whether they're lost or just late — simply because you might not have communicated clearly enough in your directions.

It's hardly fair to keep a client in the dark simply by neglecting to explain to him what you're trying to accomplish. Rather than complain to the other guides about how ignorant your client is, communicate with that client. Instruct him as you go. That's what he's paying for.

Confidence

A guide can hardly expect to win the clients' confidence if he isn't confident in himself. Granted, it's always difficult to be confident in matters beyond your control. But if proper communication has taken place ahead-of-time, the client will fully understand that factors such as weather, game activity and success rates can't be guaranteed. That client does expect his guide to be competent, and therefore confident, however.

A guide has to show confidence in his own ability to make the best of whatever circumstances are dished out to him. He must show a positive, confident attitude that if he and his client work at it long and hard enough, the fish will decide to bite or the game will come their way. Just as a negative attitude is infectious, a guide's confidence is equally contagious.

Outfitters have sometimes complained that the new guides they hire out of schools fail to show confidence in themselves. Much of the fault

Communication with the client is crucial, beginning the moment he first arrives. Make sure all his questions are answered, and inform him what your plans are and why. A guide isn't doing his job if he's left his client in the dark.

there probably lies with the outfitter, though. Sending a brand new guide out with a client who is probably more experienced, and has paid a plenty big price for the hunt, into country the guide is barely familiar with is inviting trouble. But every guide must start somewhere, and the one who is confident in himself will be the one who gives his clients what they came for.

It would be difficult even for an experienced guide to feel totally confident out in territory that's new to him. He knows the success of a high-priced hunt can ride heavily on how well he knows the country. However, if two equally new guides were thrust into the same situation, the one who approached the situation with confidence would win the client's trust and have a better chance of success. The guide who worried more about his inexperience showing through would probably look inexperienced.

I once nearly lost out on a chance to run a semi-guided drop camp because the outfitter felt I was too quiet or reserved. He wanted his camp boss to exude confidence in an outgoing way — to inspire the hunters' confidence when they began to doubt the quality of the hunting or the abundance of game.

It's one thing to be confident in yourself. It's another thing to demonstrate that confidence in such a way that your client will catch it as well. That brand of confidence is essential in a guide.

The Right Image

Naturally, confidence is only part of the image a guide must convey. The way you come across to people in your actions, attitude, speech and appearance will oftentimes tell them a lot about you — including the extent of your experience. The image you convey will directly affect your relationship with the clients and your ability to deal with them effectively.

While first impressions aren't always correct, the fact remains that they last. They often set the tone for your dealings with the client. A sloppy or slovenly appearance will hardly command anybody's respect, and an attempt to convey a phony image is something both co-workers and clients will quickly see through. But at the same time, a guide who genuinely looks the part will have his client's confidence from the start.

There are limits to how much you can (or should even try to) consciously affect your image as a guide. But a western guide should look like a western guide, just as a Maine whitetail guide should look

Are these "guests" to you, or just "clients" or "dudes?" Your attitude toward the clientele you serve will show through in your dealings with them. Tact is an absolute must. (Photo courtesy Rob Johnson)

like he belongs in the northern woods, etc. Clients do expect their guides to look the part.

However, the fact that clients like to see local color doesn't mean you should put on a show. I've seen brand new western guides dress more like Hollywood actors or Nashville singers than like people who actually make their living out in the backcountry. Unfortunately, clients can usually tell the difference right off the bat as well.

A distinct regional accent such as one from the South or East may immediately brand you as a non-native of the region you're working in. But that's not much to worry about. I know a Montana packer who has a strong Pennsylvania accent, but otherwise he comes across as just one of the locals. And as a guide he would put most of the locals to shame. In the end, its what you do, not how you talk or dress, that will show your true color as a guide.

Again, a sloppy image will hardly command respect, and a phony one will bring outright disdain. It's best to just blend in with the locals you're working with and not get too image-conscious beyond that. Experience will take care of the rest. The right image is important, but it's best to look the part by being the part.

Tact

An outfitter's wife recently told me about the new crew they had hired for the year. They were working out well, but one brand-new guide still had some things to learn. For example, when fitting saddles to the new hunting clients that had arrived at the trailhead, the young guide told one of them, "This saddle should fit you pretty well. We had a little short guy on it last week."

That ain't tact. True, having always been short-statured, the hunter probably took it in stride. He might have even been amused by the blunder. The guide had all good intentions, and it was an honest mistake on his part. But he could have offended the client. A guide *has* to think before he acts or speaks. Tactfulness is crucial in your dealings with clients.

An insightful hunter once told me that guides hold a real mystique in their clients' eyes. (Maybe that mystique is what makes you want to become a guide.) However, too many guides look down their noses at clients as a result. They talk down to their clients, or at best criticize and laugh at them behind their backs. (And believe me, clients will give you no end of things to laugh and/or complain about.) Rather than looking down on your client because of his inabilities or inexperience, strive to elevate that client, at least in his own mind, to your level.

You will notice that I frequently use the term "client," and occasionally even "dude," when referring to those who enlist the services of a guide. However, I use those terms only to make a point or to avoid confusion, as the context dictates. A wise outfitter taught me early-on that the term "guest" is much more desirable. It helps keep your attitude positive when referring to that clientele, and it also reminds you that you're dealing with more than a mere business relationship.

I once heard of an English woman who was asked to describe her experience of having met with two prominent members of Parliament. The first one, she said, had made her feel as if she were with the most important person in all the world. The second one, however, had made her feel as if *she* were the most important person in the world. The second one had an understanding of tact.

Maybe that's carrying things a bit far in the case of guides. However,

Dealing with an increasingly know- ledgeable public, a guide must learn continually — either from experience, from other guides, or from published material. If you don't want to be a student, you'd best not become a guide.

guides should at least treat their clients as equals. A guide who is an excellent hunter or fisherman but can't deal tactfully with his clients will probably lose more business than he brings back.

Constant Learning

If you want to become a guide because you don't want to use your head, you're choosing the wrong occupation. The recreation industry is becoming increasingly competitive, and much of its clientele is changing. Also, the public resources on which much of the guiding industry depends are becoming entangled in more and more bureaucracy, red tape, management policies and regulation. Anyone who wants to keep ahead in the business must be a constant student of new (and old) developments.

Also, there has been a proliferation of outdoor magazines and sportsman/conservation groups along with growing outdoor interest amongst the "non-consumptive" public. This has resulted in heavy competition to come out with the latest information on ecology, game biology and management, or the latest scoop on new hunting products and techniques. As a result, guides are dealing with a more and more informed public. Every guide has to be something of a student even to stay abreast of new developments, much less to stay ahead of the people he'll be guiding.

One simplistic example of this is the fairly recent development and exploding popularity of cow elk calls. For years no one thought twice about the sounds that cow elk make. Few people were even aware of those vocalizations. However, one enterprising hunter began to realize their significance, and he soon mass-produced a commercial call to mimic those sounds.

Hunters nationwide took note and began making use of those calls. Any elk guide who failed to stay abreast of this new development missed out on an effective hunting technique. He also found himself less knowledgeable than some of the hunters he guided. The same can often happen when it comes to new behavioral or biological discoveries or theories regarding fish or game.

A guide must also be a student in areas other than book knowledge. A day should never pass in which a guide doesn't learn something new and catalog it in his mind for future use. It may be a bit of local history (which is often important to the clients), some new land feature he's happened onto in his hunting territory, some habit of the fish or game he guides for, or even some observation of human nature in the clients he deals with.

A guide must constantly catalog bits of information he hears from other guides, hunters, or packers, as well as filing away his own observations. Eventually, those bits of information he has filed away in his memory will fall together and pay off. For example, one of the first elk I put a client onto was taken partly because I had listened to my employer and borrowed a tactic from him.

After picking up tracks and determining that we were trailing a bull, I determined from the warmth of the droppings that we were very close behind him. I had heard my boss speak of putting the hunter out in front in situations like that, and it made sense. Before long, my hunter raised his rifle and dropped a bull that he wouldn't have gotten a shot at if I had been in front of him on the track. Studying what worked for other guides certainly paid off there.

Horse Sense/Woods Sense/People Sense

Maybe some folks would refer to this simply as a sixth sense. I'm not sure it's something that can be consciously developed the way other character traits can be. It seems that some folks just have a natural feel for who or what they are dealing with — an ability to read or sense what lies beneath the surface.

However, I do believe this trait can always be cultivated to some extent simply through experience and observation. Experience with the folks and critters and situations you'll deal with as a guide is certainly the best way to develop a feel for them. No one is such a natural that he gains savvy without experience. But even that experience is worthless without an ability to observe and understand — to read the circumstances and situations you're dealing with. What it really all boils down to, again, is common sense.

I once guided a couple of hunters up into a basin where we often saw deer or elk. Most of the way there (several miles) we were working

The more experience you have, the more credibility you'll have as a guide. Experience is the main qualification for the job. But if you lack experience, don't lose heart. Everyone must start somewhere.

through crusted snow that showed nothing but frozen-in elk tracks from the evening before. However, a few years earlier I had seen several nice bucks feeding in the basin after a similar snow pushed them down from a high rock rim up above. I was confident I would find them there again.

My hunters had seen nothing in the way of fresh sign and were beginning to think I was wasting their time. But based on past experience and observation, I more than just thought we had a good chance of seeing deer. Somehow, I knew — I could feel it — that we would get into deer. I came out of the situation pretty well when both of the hunters got five-point bucks. That's the best way I can describe that extra sense.

Experience

Experience will take care of a lot of the problems you may encounter early in a guiding career. It's only through experience that you will gain most of the knowledge, confidence, woods sense and savvy that a guide really needs. In fact, without a great deal of experience you're really not ready to be a guide.

That's right, without a good bit of experience with the fish or game species you're guiding for, the type of country you're working in, the firearms, archery gear or fishing tackle your clients are using, or even the horses, snowmobiles or cross-country skis you'll be using, you can hardly expect to be savvy in every situation you'll encounter with a paying guest. You'll need experience at dealing with all different types of people as well. In reality, without that extensive experience, you're not fully qualified to be a guide.

But don't lose heart. The only way to gain experience at those things is by doing them, and the best way to do that is to get yourself into a position where you *can* do them. Unless you live in an area where you can get that experience, or are able to move there, it may mean simply hiring on with an outfitter who is willing and able to give you that experience.

Ideally, a guide should have several years experience at hunting, fishing, etc., in the area where he will be working. However, the demand for guides often requires that they be brought in from other areas, sometimes on short notice. That's why so many guide schools have sprung up. In today's urbanized society experienced guides are difficult to come by, so many new guides have to simply gain their experience — and sometimes even much of their initial training — on the job.

When an outfitter hires you as a guide, he is obligated (if not by law, at least by ethics) to get you well familiarized with his territory and the game you will be hunting. If you have little or no experience hunting what his clients come for, he may use you as a packer or campjack until you've gained sufficient experience to guide a paying client.

Even at that, in your first season or two you may end up guiding clients who have more experience than you do. The only real way to get beyond that uneasy situation is to get a few years' experience under your belt and learn as much as you can along the way.

It's virtually impossible to come across like a seasoned guide if you're not one. You won't appear experienced without experience. But don't let that discourage you. Every guide had to start somewhere, and the best way to get there is to get yourself into a position to begin gaining that experience and to learn from those who have already been there.

If it's any consolation, outfitter Jerry Malson, who is becoming a leader in guide training, has said that many times the best guides he has seen are those who started out hunting whitetails, pheasants, coons and cottontails in the farmlots and woodlots far from where they intend to become a guide. You can start learning the fundamentals and developing an outdoor savvy wherever you are. The rest you can learn when you get there.

A guide must have an intimate knowledge of his area as well as the game and other wildlife it sustains. Every possible opportunity should be spent scouting, during off-seasons as well as pre-season. Quality optics are as essential for scouting as for actual hunting.

CHAPTER THREE

RESPONSIBILITIES OF A GUIDE

I once worked briefly with a would-be guide who made very little effort to get acquainted with the country in which he would be working. Even while the outfitter had his crew and summer guests in his hunting area, the guide simply used his free time and lay-over days to stay in camp and read. Besides not scouting on his own, he opted not to even go out on day-rides with the guests into country he had not yet seen. That guide was replaced within two weeks.

By now you've probably figured out that while guiding is a great way of life, it's hardly mere fun and games. It involves an awful lot of responsibility. A guide is responsible for the physical safety of himself and his clients as well as whatever crew he's working with. He's also responsible for any equipment belonging to the outfitter or the clients, and he's largely responsible for the success of the clients' outing.

All that amounts to quite a load riding on a guide's shoulders. And it's not a load to be taken lightly. No two guides would categorize their responsibilities the same way, but here's a more specific break-down that pretty well covers the bases.

Know Your Territory

This is one of the more obvious responsibilities of a guide, but it's important for more reasons than what first crosses the mind. Granted, a guide must know how to get his client into an area to hunt or fish, then get him back to camp or civilization safely and conveniently. Realistically though, most times a guide with any savvy at all could do a passable job without ever having scouted the country before.

More importantly, a guide needs to know the country well so that he can get his clients around it as quietly, quickly and effectively as possible. It's important to know the passes, game trails and other features that don't show up on maps. These make it a lot easier on your client as well as making it much easier to hike or ride with a minimum of noise or time into the area you want to reach.

Also, knowing the little nooks and crannies, the game trails, wallows, natural licks, or riffles and pools gives a guide a far better chance of showing his hunting or fishing client a successful outing. It's one thing to know the general lay of the land. It's another thing to really know that country in a way that lets you give your client his money's worth.

Realistically, it takes a guide at least two or three seasons to truly get to know his outfitter's area intimately. And during those years he'll probably run into situations where knowing some small feature within that country may have made the difference between success and a near miss on game. However, a guide can always better his odds by first studying topographic maps of the area meticulously, then getting out and scouting the area every chance he gets.

A season or two ago, due to unexpected circumstances, an outfitter had to transfer a packer out of one of his camps for a week. He moved me into that camp to fill in. There happened to be a couple of clients in camp who were paying a lower rate for an "unguided" hunt. On a couple of days when I wasn't tending to packing chores, I did what I could to better these hunters' chances of scoring on elk.

Although I knew the lay of the land, I had never had a chance to scout or hunt in that area, and therefore I didn't know it intimately. On the last day of the hunt I did my best to guide one of these hunters but managed to get him into a nasty patch of deadfall I was unaware of. We got a look at elk, but no shots. And by the time I got the hunter out of that hopeless tangle of blow-downs he was too exhausted to hunt anymore.

That client was grateful for my effort (it was a service he hadn't paid for), but because I hadn't been able to learn the country ahead-of-time I ended up getting him into a jackpot that cost him his last few hours of hunting time. When guiding a client, it's imperative that a guide *know the country.*

Know the Game

It should go without saying that a guide should have an intimate knowledge of the game or fish species he pursues. He needs to be a virtual student of the game. Experience is by far the best teacher, and almost the only real teacher.

Unfortunately, would-be guides are faced with the age-old dilemma: "How can I get experience unless someone is willing to hire me?" Unless you live in an area where you can get that experience on your own, it's tough. But there are ways you can hedge the bet in your favor. "Hitting the books" is one way.

Granted, the fundamentals of hunting are basically the same for any game species: stay quiet, stay out of sight, and above all keep the wind in your favor. The same is true with fishing: once you've learned to read a stream, mastered the basics of spin- or fly-casting, and gotten the hang of twitching a lure or drifting a fly just right, those basics will be the same just about anywhere.

However, just as knowing the intimate details of your territory can make the difference between success and near misses, knowing the specific quirks and habits of the particular fish or game you're after can make the difference between sending your clients home with meat and just sending them home with memories.

Again, a guide must be a literal student of the game. When not in the field, pay plenty of attention to what experienced outdoorsmen have published in books and magazines. Publishers survive by competing to give their readers any new tip or discovery they can find to make them more knowledgeable and successful. A would-be guide is foolish not to take advantage of the wealth of knowledge that's readily available nowadays.

A lot of what is published in outdoor magazines is frequently regarded to be less than realistic or accurate. However, while not every writer is an expert hunter himself (though it's always difficult not to portray oneself as such), many still pass on solid information they've gained from those who actually have learned much by experience and success. There's plenty that a potential guide can learn from magazines and especially from books.

A few years ago a writer mentioned the common tendency of spooked elk to circle uphill, then stop and watch their back trail. Although I had encountered that several times myself, it never actually registered as a useful piece of knowledge until another experienced hunter/writer pointed it out. I later found it useful when guiding hunters.

It's also a wise idea for any guide to learn to keep his mouth shut and his ears open and just listen to other experienced guides or outdoorsmen.

I was fortunate to spend my first five years in this business working for an outfitter who loved to educate by sharing his experiences around a campfire or in the cook tent. I learned a lot about tracking elk as well as many aspects of dealing with clients simply by listening to the details in stories he told.

Even the most experienced guide never stops learning. If he does, he'd better think about a new career, because those who are more innovative and willing to learn will soon have his clients. For example, as mentioned in chapter two, a man living near Yellowstone National Park realized the elk he watched all winter communicated in more ways than just bugling. He developed a call that imitated the sounds made by cows and calves.

Within the next few years the new cow calls had made big changes in elk hunting. Before long, any guide who hadn't kept abreast of this new development was at something of a disadvantage. Other guides had

In many situations a guide will need topographic maps and a quality compass, plus a knowledge of how to read and use them. The GPS (Global Positioning System) devices now on the market may also prove quite useful, if not essential, on a guide's gear list. (Photo courtesy Bob Ward and Sons, Inc.)

found how effective the new-fangled calls could be, and elk-hunting clients expected their guides to know how to use them effectively. The same happened recently with grunt and bleat calls for deer.

Although few realistic hunting or fishing tactics are truly "new," any guide must stay abreast of those that are found to be effective. And even the old, time-tested tactics are worth a would-be guide's research. A guide *must* know the game his clients hire him to pursue. He must continually be a student of that game.

Know the Regulations and the Biology Behind Them

For obvious reasons, it's crucial that a guide know the local, state and federal regulations governing hunting, fishing or whatever else he's guiding for. He could cost the client(s) as well as himself a good bit of money in fines, etc., by breaking the regulations either deliberately or in ignorance. He could also jeopardize his employer's entire business through ignorance of certain laws, especially federal game laws.

Outfitter Smoke Elser feels it is also important that a guide have some understanding of the biological principles behind those regulations. Folks in the outfitting industry must always be aware that what we're dealing with is a sustainable and renewable resource. With a growing human population, the demands upon those natural resources is continually increasing, and a guide with little understanding of the biology of the resource will be limited in his understanding of how best to use it without destroying it. He'll also have difficulty passing the necessity of wise use on to the clients he deals with.

Know The History and Natural History of the Region

Along the same line, Elser feels a guide must have a good knowledge of all the flora and fauna of the area where he's guiding — not just the game or fish he's after. Occasionally a guide will deal with someone who is there only to catch big fish or shoot lots of game. However, whether they realize it or not, even the "consumptive" clients are paying a guide for more than just getting them into good fishing or getting game animals into their sights.

Flowers may not do much for your adrenaline flow, but as a guide you'll find that the clients you deal with will often be fascinated by wildflowers and other vegetation. And you'll find that the more you learn about the various trees, brush species and other vegetation, the more you will understand how various game species use and depend on those

A guide must know more than just how to find game animals for clients. Knowing all his area's flora and fauna and their interrelationships will make him a more complete and competent guide. And understanding the biology behind the regulations and management policies will make him a better steward of the resource.

various plants.

Clients will also be full of questions about birds and other wildlife, from camp jays to eagles, from squirrels to marten to wolverines. The guide who has a knowledge of all the wildlife in his area will be far more likely to win his clients' confidence than the one who can present nothing more than a few basics on what game or fish he's after.

The same goes for knowing the history of the area where you guide. Every region has its own history, legend and tradition. The more of it a guide can pass on, the better. Again, even though they don't always realize it, most clients who hire a guide are looking for something of that local flavor.

Have The Right Equipment and Know How To Use It

It's plenty possible to get by without all the gadgets and trimmings many people think they need. But there are also times when the success of a client's trip may depend on the quality of the guide's gear. A guide who allows himself to be limited in some way by his gear (poor-quality binoculars or spotting scope, for example) may be cheating his clients.

Also, the quality (or lack of it) of a guide's equipment can have a big influence on the impression he makes on his client — and on how much confidence the client then places in that guide. Granted, no guide can "buy" a seasoned image simply by spending money on expensive gear. Clients will see right through that. However, quality equipment will reflect the professionalism and knowledge that come with experience. Clients will sense when their guide is dedicated enough to lay out what it takes to get the right gear because he knows by experience what

For a hunting guide, the difference between quality optics and poor ones can mean the difference between success and failure. Gear is a big expense for most guides, but they must have the right equipment. When a client pays good money for your services, you owe it to him to have the right stuff. (Photo courtesy Bob Ward & Sons, Inc)

works.

A guide's living expenses are usually minimal when he's in the back-country. Unfortunately though, a lot of his wages may end up going to buy necessary gear. A guide's work is plenty tough on clothes, and quality footgear will be a seemingly constant expense for any guide whose job requires much footwork. (A guide owes it to his client to be outfitted with boots that will get him into the slickest, nastiest areas and keep him comfortable and eager to do his job. As much footwork as most hunting guides must do, they would be foolish to be chincy when it comes to boots.)

Naturally, the gear guides need varies from one region to another and from one outfit to another. Some outfitters provide saddles for their guides, while others expect a guide to furnish his own saddle, saddlebags and scabbard (if he carries a rifle). While some outfitters won't allow their guides to carry a firearm, others expect them to in case they need to bring down game a client has wounded (more on that later). In vast, open country a guide will often need a spotting scope. However, in many

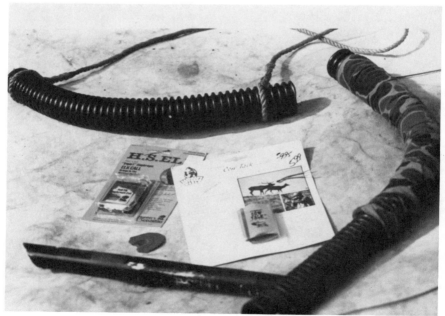

A few examples of the many elk calls on the market. Again, a guide owes it to his clients to find what works in his area, then make sure he has the right gear and knows how to use it.

thickly timbered areas a scope would be virtually useless.

The list could go on and on. Elk bugles, flashlights, camo clothing, fishing waders, you name it. One of the few constants, of course, is that any guide (at least a hunting guide) will need a quality binocular. The other is that quality gear will be a major and constant expense. But it will be a reflection on your commitment, as well as your experience, as a guide.

It's usually best to wait to stock up on most gear until you have landed a job and had a chance to see what works best in that particular area. What you can count on, though, is that a guide must have the right equipment, and he must know how to use it. Again, your client's success may ride on it.

As a footnote, perhaps the gear more universally essential than even good binoculars is a reasonably good camera and a knowledge of basic photography. Every client will want photos of his big fish — especially if he plans to release them — or his big buck, bull or other game.

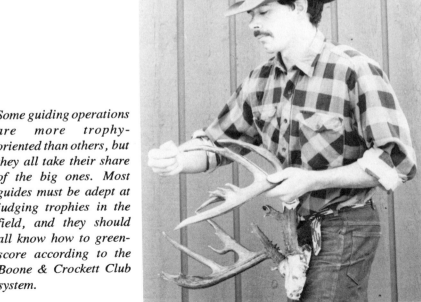

Some guiding operations are more trophy-oriented than others, but they all take their share of the big ones. Most guides must be adept at judging trophies in the field, and they should all know how to green-score according to the Boone & Crockett Club system.

Excellent field care once game is on the ground is top priority for a guide. He must be able to get the animal dressed, skinned, caped and cooled, then pack it out without ruining trophies or meat. (Photo courtesy Wildlife Adventures, Inc.)

Sooner or later a client will forget his camera or simply leave it in camp because he doesn't want to pack the extra weight around. They'll all depend on you to take "hero shots" of them, even with their own cameras.

Compact cameras that take high-quality photos are readily available, and the basics of getting good snapshots are simple and easy to master. Every guide should have one and know how to compose good photos.

Trophy And Meat Care

Depending on an outfitter's location, the size and quality of game populations in his area, and the type of clients he caters to, he may or may not be a "trophy" outfitter. Those who do offer trophy hunting or trophy fishing will likely charge a higher fee, and they'll expect more from their guides.

A guide working for such an operation will be responsible for knowing how to score trophies according to the Boone & Crockett Club's system or some similar scoring system. He'll also need to become adept at judging trophies in the field.

Even the less trophy-oriented outfits will take trophy-sized fish or game animals from time to time. And many hunters or fishermen will consider even the smaller ones to be trophies. A trophy is in the eye of the beholder, which means every guide will need to know how to cape, flesh and salt game heads or keep fish in good condition for the taxidermist.

A guide is also responsible for keeping his client's meat in good condition — clean as well as cool, unspoiled and free of flies. In some situations he may be able to load the game whole into a vehicle or over a pack animal, and then take it straight to a butcher or at least hang it in camp to be skinned and cooled out.

However, in most backcountry situations a guide will have to know how to skin and quarter an animal, or bone the meat, then get the meat cooled out and packed back to camp without leaving the client a tainted, dirty mess.

Know The Clients' Gear and How To Use It

Although the guide is not the one doing the shooting, flycasting, or whatever the case may be, he still must oftentimes know the client's gear better than the client does. Granted, it's the client's responsibility to become competent with his choice of gear before he arrives for a hunting or fishing trip. Realistically, however, if the client were that competent he wouldn't need to hire a guide.

True, some of the more competent clients do hire outfitters mainly for other services, such as providing horses, packers, and boats or other equipment. But one of the main services a client pays for is the guide's expertise and coaching. That includes general familiarity with his gear. Once the guide puts the client onto fish or game, he has to be able to advise the client as to how to hook it or put it on the ground.

Few of us will ever be true technical experts on firearms and ballistics, archery tackle, or even fishing gear and lures. There is simply too much for anyone other than an industry expert to stay abreast of. But I've encountered would-be guides and even active guides who know less in those areas than the average client does. That's where trouble starts.

A fishing guide owes it to his client to have a pretty broad knowledge of various types of tackle and casting techniques, plus *when* they work best, and *why*. Any hunting guide had better know a fair bit about archery, pistols, muzzleloaders or centerfire rifles, whichever his client

Not every client will be competent with his own gear. Few guides will be all-around technical experts, but they must at least be competent enough to help novice clients make good use of their equipment. (Photo courtesy Scott Boulanger)

is using. He has to know what problems his clients may encounter, how close he must get them to their game, and where they should aim under various field conditions.

A guide dealing with firearms hunters must at least have a basic familiarity with the various rifle and pistol cartridges and their relative merits and limitations. He should know basic ballistic principles — at least enough that he can consult a ballistics table and make sensible mental notes on the cartridge his client is using.

A guide must know how to get his client properly sighted in at the range, then be able to coach him on how to get an accurate shot off under various field conditions. He must be able to estimate ranges accurately and make sure his client shoots only within the limits of the cartridge he's using.

Sometimes hunters are great at hitting targets from a bench rest, but then they go to pieces when shooting at game. You won't always know which ones they are. But when you see a client shoot poorly at the range before his hunt, you know he won't do any better in the field. And you'll

The limited ballistics of muzzleloaders and handguns place extra constraints on a guide. Again, he must know the client's gear at least well enough to tailor his tactics to its unique challenges. (Photo courtesy Scott Boulanger.)

Sighting in before a hunt lets a guide see how well his client is capable of shooting. He can then make specific mental notes on the rifle's caliber, ballistics, and where it's zeroed. He can also make note of any flinching or other problems he needs to coach the client through when shooting at game. (Photo courtesy Wildlife Adventures, Inc.)

know you have to coach him through each shot. It's best to be safe and coach every hunter when it comes time to shoot.

More than once I've been tipped off when hunters shot erratically at the range. By reminding them of such simple basics as relaxing, using a rest, and knowing where their sights are when they squeeze the trigger, I've been rewarded by seeing those clients get game they would otherwise have missed.

The reward is in knowing I've fulfilled my responsibility as a guide — a service that even the client may not realize he's paid for. In the end, it's up to the client to set the hook or make an accurate shot. But a guide must know how to coach that client when it gets right down to the moment of truth.

Diplomacy

At the beginning of this chapter I mentioned that one of a guide's main responsibilities is the success and well being of the client. But that's not enough. It's plenty well possible to take a client hunting or fishing or sight-seeing safely and successfully — to get him into plenty of great country and onto plenty of fish or game — and still send him home feeling like he was treated poorly or was given lousy service.

It should go without saying that every client should be treated with complete courtesy — always the way you would want to be treated yourself. And I've already pointed out that a guide must always go the extra mile. However, guides also have an ulterior motive. Return business is crucial to the success of most guiding operations, so a guide has an extra incentive to treat every client well and do his best for that client.

When you hire on with an outfitter, you're automatically committing yourself to do your absolute best for him — and for his clients — just as with any employer. When you bring in repeat business for the outfitter, you're also ensuring your own future employment.

In the end, your responsibility is always to do your best for the clients and treat them diplomatically, even when they make it seem impossible. But if you need extra incentive, remember you're benefitting yourself by bringing return clientele.

Take Top Care of the Outfitter's Gear and Stock

I know of a former guide who arrived at the trailhead with a pickup load of hay and claimed to have set a new speed record for the time it took him to make the 70-mile drive. I never worked directly with that guide, but I'm well familiar with the curving, winding, bumpy, pot-hole-filled dirt road that he had just driven up.

Given the risk to the outfitter's vehicle, the beating that vehicle took, and the chance of losing the outfitter's hay, it would be safe to call that guide foolish. For various reasons he didn't last long with that outfit and was not invited to return.

When an outfitter hires a crew, he needs to be able to delegate many different tasks to them. He simply can't supervise every guide every minute. He must be able to trust them with his stock and gear, and it's every guide's responsibility to treat that outfitter's gear as if it were his own.

An outfitter's "bread and butter" — his whole ability to serve clients and make a living — is tied up in the livestock, vehicles, camp gear, boats, rafts, or whatever other equipment he uses. A guide carries a heavy load of responsibility any time he uses any of that gear, or is put in charge of caring for and maintaining it.

That fact was best brought home to me one time when a client got to asking about the pack string I was pulling from camp site to camp site on a summer pack/fishing trip. The outfitter told the guest that, between the value of the horses and mules I was leading, the saddles, and the camp gear, I was in charge of well over $10,000 worth of stock and equipment. I realized then more than ever that although I thoroughly loved and enjoyed my job as a packer and guide, I really did carry a big load on my shoulders.

True, some equipment can occasionally be replaced or repaired on fairly short notice — but rarely without a large expense and certainly not without costly inconvenience. Enough problems arise through normal wear and tear or unavoidable accidents without a guide neglecting to care for his boss' gear.

There are plenty of ways a negligent guide can cost his employer dearly. It may be a carelessly driven stock truck, a poorly serviced or maintained shuttle vehicle, or a horse sored up through sloppy saddling or packing. It may be carelessly packed client duffel, or even poorly cared-for groceries (that have been carefully allotted to last through an

A neat, clean, well organized tack room is one example of how a guide should care for his employer's gear. An outfitter's whole livelihood is invested in his stock, vehicles and equipment.

eight- or ten-day trip).

Any number of things can cost an outfitter a great deal of money, either in lost business or in refunds for services he couldn't make good on — not to mention the loss of the stock or equipment itself. All because a guide neglected to take responsibility.

Ethics

I'll deal more in depth with this topic in Chapter Seven, but it bears mentioning here. Naturally, a guide is responsible for staying within the laws and regulations that govern the industry and resources he deals with. But ethics deal with more than just what laws and regulations require.

As often as not ethics deal with areas the law doesn't specifically cover, such as how you treat your livestock or deal with your clients or impact natural resources when no one is watching. They also include staying within laws and limits when you know you could get away with breaking them. Guides are often tempted to overstep ethical bounds in order to further their own success rates. However, such guides often give the entire industry a bad name. (Again, more on that in Chapter Seven.)

Occasionally guides may face difficult ethical dilemmas. One example is the question alluded to earlier of whether or not he should bring down game a client has wounded. There may come a time when a client makes a poor shot and it becomes obvious he's not capable of keeping up the pace or covering the country necessary to track down and dispatch an animal he has wounded. The law says it's illegal for anyone else to shoot his game for him. Ethics say it's wrong to let that animal escape and suffer a slow death. What should a guide do?

Naturally, ethics also dictate that a guide should never let the client take a risky shot in the first place. However, assuming an animal were wounded anyway, most would agree that when the client is no longer physically capable, his guide is ethically bound to pursue and dispatch that game himself even though it would technically be illegal. In so doing, the guide assumes whatever legal consequences may befall him, but he must do what is ethically right.

Most ethical questions are more clear-cut for a guide. But whatever the situation, he is responsible to act ethically in all his dealings.

Positive Attitude, Hard Work, and Commitment

Although these have already been touched on as well, they also bear discussion again here. These qualities are not just characteristics that would be nice to find in a guide; they're responsibilities.

As I attempted to describe earlier, circumstances will rarely be favorable no matter what you're trying to accomplish as a guide. Whether you're dealing with lousy weather, lack of appropriate tools, poor hunting or fishing, a client you can't stand to be around, or some other form of poor working conditions, it's your job as a guide to make the absolute best of it.

Look for whatever needs done, pitch in and do it without being asked, and work hard at it. Get the job done no matter what. And keep a positive attitude and a smile as you go the extra mile. That's minimum requirement for a guide.

When an outfitter turns you loose with a drift boat, a vehicle, a string of mules loaded with camp gear, or with his clients, can he trust you with that responsibility? (Photo courtesy Scott Boulanger)

CHAPTER FOUR

DEALING WITH THE CLIENT

During the entire two-hour drive from the trailhead and corrals down to the outfitter's home place, the hunter riding in the pickup with me complained. Although he didn't grouse about me or anything I'd done, I could tell his discontent was directed **at** me. Finally, his partner tried to quiet him down.

The malcontent client had just come off a hunt in which he took a five-point bull elk and a four-point mule deer. Although neither was of trophy proportions, the hunter should have been quite happy with his results. Obviously something had been handled poorly.

Part of the problem was that the hunter had filled his tags three days into a ten-day hunt. Although he arrived a day late (due to a government-imposed forest closure) and chose to leave a day early, he still had five days in which to get bored. He had a restless, nervous personality, and his boredom soon turned to agitation, then to outright irritation. Mole hills grew into mountains in his idle mind.

However, the real source of the problem was a mistake I had made as his guide. I had mishandled a situation that eventually came to be the source of his discontentment. He didn't return as a client.

The Perfect Hunter/Fisherman

Before I describe the incident further, let me make a few equally important points on dealing with clients. The first is that it's important for a guide to have reasonable expectations. All too often a guide sets his expectations too high. He wants the client to be just as capable and competent at hunting, fishing, riding or hiking around the country as the guide himself is.

It does little good to waste time complaining about a client's quirks, clumsiness, or lack of ability. If your clients were as capable as you wish they were, they wouldn't need guides in the first place (and you would be out of a job).

A guide should try to bring out the client's highest potential, and that may sometimes mean pushing that client to his utmost limit. However, in order to really succeed in giving clients what they come for, a guide must learn to deal with them on their level, within their capabilities.

Don't waste time wishing for the perfect client. You'll never find him.

The Essence of Guiding

While preparing to write this book, I asked several outfitters what they felt should be covered in a book for prospective guides. Naturally, each of them emphasized the relationship between the guide and his client, and each viewed it from the perspective of working with a client who is less than perfect.

Former outfitter Roland Cheek phrased the idea especially well when he said, "It may be easy for *you* to go out and get a big buck, but it isn't near as easy to take a hunter who's out of shape and can't walk quietly and can't see game very well and get him onto a big buck. To me, that's *the essence of guiding*."

The same goes for guiding inept fishermen, trail riders, or any other kind of "dude." The less competent the client is, the greater challenge you face as a guide.

One of the few disadvantages of being a guide is that you may get little chance to actually hunt or fish yourself. But that drawback is often countered with the argument that you should find just as much satisfaction in the greater challenge of getting that second person — who is often totally inept — into a position to get what he came for.

Don't get the negative idea that all clients will be inept klutzes that guides hate to deal with. Yet all too many guides fail to see the real challenge in guiding. They frustrate themselves wishing for the perfect client or complaining because they haven't found him. But most often the real satisfaction in guiding comes from helping those less competent clients succeed.

One of the most memorable experiences from my years as a guide is the morning I took a 69-year-old man out on horseback and got him

Guiding Dad, one of the highlights of the author's career. But even guiding your life-long hunting partner has its challenges. Too many guides wish for the ideal client. They'll never find him.

into position to shoot a six-point bull elk. The hunter had gone through cataract surgery on both eyes as well as a triple heart-bypass operation just the year before. He missed getting a shot off at the bull by just a split second, but it was satisfying just to know I had gotten him that close. If he had gotten the bull, I'm sure I would count it my greatest success as a guide.

The "essence of guiding" is far more than just going out and showing clients what you do well. It involves taking people with less skill, knowledge, physical ability and experience — and sometimes folks with basically none at all — and helping *them* do what comes easily for you. And it involves giving those clients something more to take home than just the tangible trophies they came for — getting them to see more than just antler points or pounds of fish. True guiding involves helping clients to grasp the entire experience to the fullest.

Psychology

When discussing this project with outfitters, I also frequently heard

"The Essence of Guiding." Taking a client whose ability is limited in some way, and helping him meet the challenges of doing what comes easily for you: that's what guiding is all about.

them mention the word "psychology." Although it's crucial that a guide be able to get his client onto the fish or game he's after, the psychology of the guide/client relationship is undoubtedly the most important part of guiding.

A guide must understand the client and what makes him tick. That's what enables him to tailor his efforts to that client's personality and abilities. It's also what makes for success in dealing with each client. Outfitter Smoke Elser refers to this as the social aspect of the guide/client relationship.

I once got a good lesson from a client's perspective as I guided Mike Post, a long-time client and eastern representative of Roland Cheek's Skyline Outfit. Mike has a particularly good insight into such matters, and as we ate lunch out on a mountainside, he told me, "Every hunter thinks he's the baddest man in the woods, but when he gets out here, you guides hold a real mystique. He'll do anything you say."

That image is a big part of what many clients are paying for in a guide (more on that later). And because guides do hold such a mystique for most clients, it's important that they understand the psychological aspect of dealing with each client. No two will fit the same mold.

The psychology of any client you'll deal with is affected by his physical condition, mental attitude, and emotions or personality. A guide has to learn to read his client in each of these areas and deal with each one accordingly. For example, when Mike Post told me most hunters will do anything a guide says, he also told me that an outfitter once said to him, "I've learned that when my hunters stop talking to me, it's time to start hunting back toward camp."

That outfitter had learned to read how mentally and physically tired his hunters were by how much they talked to him. They wouldn't come right out and tell him.

Fairly early in my guiding career I got a mild chewing-out from the outfitter for keeping my hunters out too long. I had developed a reputation for getting into camp late, and when I took some razzing over it, I defended myself by commenting that I simply waited for them to tell me they wanted to go back to camp. The outfitter's wife insightfully said, "But they don't want to admit that to a 23-year-old guide." I had failed to read them.

Outfitter Jerry Malson calls this interrelationship "Client Leadership Management." As he teaches his guide-school students, "The guide sets the drumbeat. He can set the client up a step and motivate him, or he can set the client down." And just as with the client I mentioned at the start of the chapter, down is exactly the direction the client's morale will go when the guide fails to understand and deal with him appropriately.

For several years in a row, one of the outfitters I've worked for had a repeat client that the entire crew found difficult to deal with. Although he tried to be good-natured overall, this particular hunter tended to be gruff, outspoken and demanding. He never seemed satisfied no matter how good our efforts were, and none of us could figure out just how to keep him happy.

Then one year a guide who was brand-new to the outfit ran up against this hard-to-please client. Rather than let himself be "buffaloed," he hit the hunter with a relentless barrage of ribbing. The hunter loved it. He was entirely easier to deal with from then on. Apparently what he had wanted all along was just to be "one of the boys." His demanding attitude had just been his attempt to mold the camp into a setting where he felt he fit in.

Whether by accident or design, that brand new guide had found a rather unorthodox way to keep a difficult client happy. The rest of us had tried to do our best for that client, but we had failed to hit on what he was really looking for. Even the best efforts can fall short when a guide fails to read the client and understand the psychological aspect of

To an experienced elk hunter, that trickle of urine leading from the elk's bed confirms that you're tracking a bull. To many clients it means absolutely nothing. Taking time to teach them little things you take for granted will usually make their trip a success — regardless of whether they get game.

guiding.

Teaching

A guide can't guarantee that his client will catch all the fish he expects or get the game his heart is set on. However, a guide *can* improve the client's odds by teaching along the way. Even if the client doesn't get the fish or game he's after, he'll have something to take home with him — the knowledge he's gained. Often, that knowledge alone will leave him feeling the trip was a success.

Naturally, the more a client knows and understands, the better his odds of success. By continually teaching him what you're looking for, what you're trying to accomplish, and why you do things the way you do, you'll double your odds. Many guides make the mistake of expecting their clients to follow along blindly. Then they wonder why the client isn't ready when that fleeting opportunity comes.

I know of a case where a man booked a trip with an outfitter specifically so that outfitter could teach him how to hunt. He had never hunted in his life, and he knew from the start that he needed someone to teach him. Not every client realizes that he needs or wants to be taught. But most realize that they want to experience and learn something of what you as a guide deal with on a daily basis.

Fishing guides are often hired with the expectation that they'll teach the client how to cast, or which fly/lure/bait to use, and when. However, hunting guides must often teach without being asked. Just remember that, as mentioned earlier, outdoorsmen often feel a bit macho about themselves. So teach in a way that makes them feel more so, rather than teaching "down" to them.

Outfitter Smoke Elser has said that he's often been successful simply by having his guides spend mid-day hours teaching clients how to hunt. His guides will hunt hard during prime time — the first few hours of the morning and the last few hours of evening. Then they'll spend the slower, less productive mid-day hours looking for tracks, beds or other fresh sign while teaching the client what to look for.

As the clients learn to tell a fresh track from an old one, a cow track from a bull track, or a cow's bed from a bull's bed, they become more and more enthusiastic about putting their new-found knowledge to work. Their odds of success will improve as they learn to hunt *with* you rather than follow blindly, and they'll have something to take home with them — even if they don't get the game they're after.

Sharing the Overall Experience

Guides occasionally encounter a few clients whose entire focus is simply on how many fish they can catch or how much game they can kill. Some will measure their success only in terms of pounds of fish caught or antler spreads and point counts. But most clients seek a much broader experience, whether they actually realize it or not. They want to live a bit of the life a guide lives, and they want to sample the country he lives in.

The opportunity to share that experience is one of the few things a guide can guarantee. He can't guarantee that the weather or the game will cooperate, but he can do everything in his power to give the client a good experience. That may include sharing his knowledge of the local history or vegetation, or taking time to explain how to tie some of the knots and hitches he uses on the stock. It may mean showing the client how to saddle his own horse, or maybe just sitting on a stump and shooting the breeze with him over the campfire or in the cook tent after the day's work is done.

Several years ago at a convention of the Montana Outfitters and Guides Association, I sat in on a rap session for guides. Several outfitters also sat in, and they got to talking amongst themselves about what they really looked for in a guide. Most of them agreed that if they had to choose between a guide who was a good hunter and one who was good with people, they wouldn't hesitate to take the guide who was good with people. It's crucial that a guide be able to share the overall experience with the clients he deals with. That's what keeps them coming back.

I especially enjoyed guiding a particular client who hunted out of our elk camp for several years. On his second hunt he got a big, dark-antlered six-point bull. The following year he passed up shots at a spike and a five-point bull, even though he saw them on the last day of his hunt. When one of the guides asked why he had passed up easy shots he simply said, "I don't care about killing an elk. I just like to come up here and enjoy the camp and shoot the breeze with you guys."

Be careful though. Sharing the experience should never take the place of an honest, all-out effort to get a client onto the game or fish he came for. That's rarely the client's main goal. It makes no difference how lousy the conditions are or how worn-out or discouraged you are. Any attempt to substitute scenery or entertainment for an all-out guiding effort will probably lose the client. He'll have good reason to feel cheated.

However, like the hunter I just mentioned, most clients want more than *just* a lot of fish or dead game. Again, giving them a good overall experience is one of the few things a guide can guarantee.

Motivation

Motivation is much a part of the psychology of dealing with clients. However, it's such a big part of guiding that it merits a more specific discussion here. Keeping clients motivated when the hunting is poor or they're just plain worn out is often a guide's biggest challenge.

Realistically, a client's motivation should begin long before he arrives on the scene, but it rarely does. Few clients get into adequate physical condition. Most fail to realize what they're getting into. One of the biggest complaints among guides, even in the formal rap session mentioned earlier, was simply clients' lack of physical ability to get around the backcountry. Still, it's up to the guide to keep them motivated.

Again, as outfitter and guide-school operator Jerry Malson says, "The guide sets the drumbeat for the client. Either he can set him up a step and motivate him, or he can set him down a step." It's important for a guide to keep a positive and confident attitude himself. Often that contagious enthusiasm is the best form of motivation. Combined with a bit of discreet and timely encouragement, that enthusiasm can challenge and motivate a client to push beyond what he thinks his physical limitations are.

Moderation

One way *not* to motivate a client is to continually stay thirty paces in front of him and make him struggle to keep up. At best you'll end up with a frustrated, exhausted client who's worn out by the second day of his hunt. Worse yet, you'll probably jump game and it will be out of sight before your client ever gets in position to see it.

One of the first and hardest lessons I had to learn as a guide was to put myself in the client's boots. Even though a guide is used to the backcountry and can get around just fine, that doesn't mean the client feels that way. A guide needs to learn to feel the pain and fatigue that the client feels, or at least try to sense his limitations.

Granted, at times you do have to try to motivate that client to push beyond his own limitations. Still, that doesn't mean those limits are the same as yours. A guide must discern when to push hard, when to take a break, and when to call it a day. Motivation must be balanced with moderation, and the best way to know when to say when is to try putting yourself in the client's boots.

Communication

Nothing is more crucial to your success as a guide than your ability to communicate with the client. Quite often situations that are old hat to an experienced guide are totally foreign to the client. (Again, that's why he hired a guide.) Where you might react instinctively, the client needs to be told what to do. He needs to be informed of where you're going, what you're trying to accomplish, and what he's doing right or wrong.

All too often guides simply assume the client understands what the guide is doing or why he's doing what he is. And all too often the client needlessly gets left in the dark. If anything, it's best to assume that the client needs extra coaching. Risk over-communicating rather than fail to communicate enough.

One day a fellow guide came into camp totally disappointed and irritated at his client. As the two of them rode horseback along a high mountain ridge, a big mule deer buck rose from its bed and trotted casually out of sight. The client simply sat in the saddle and watched it disappear.

Although the shot would have been a bit long, it certainly wasn't out of the question. But rather than bail off his horse, grab his rifle from the scabbard, rest over a nearby rock, and fire, the client just sat his horse as if frozen there. While the guide would have reacted instinctively, the client needed to be told what to do. The guide failed to communicate.

Even when taking the shot, many clients need to be coached as to where to aim. They need to be reminded to concentrate on the proper sight picture and then squeeze the trigger. I've even had clients actually wait for me to tell them to go ahead and shoot, even with a big bull elk right in front of them.

One client wanted me to shoot his elk for him. But when I told him I didn't carry a rifle and that this was both wrong and illegal, he realized he would have to accomplish it himself. By simply reminding him of something so basic as knowing where his crosshairs were when he squeezed the trigger, I helped him get off a good shot and drop a decent bull. It was something most guides could easily take for granted, but something this hunter needed coaching on.

Obviously, the need for communication applies to the entire

guide/client relationship, not just shooting. It begins with getting acquainted and putting the client at ease when he first arrives in camp. And it may include matters so simple as reminding the client to grab his lunch or even his shells before leaving camp for the day.

It rarely hurts to over-communicate, even when that means reminding the client of something he doesn't need reminded of. The little misunderstandings caused by a lack of communication can cost hard-earned opportunities and lead to bigger problems.

Taking Charge

Most clients will follow their guides like dogs on a leash. But occasionally, some will have minds of their own and want to do things their own way. (Somewhere in between would be the ideal balance, but such clients are rare.) A guide needs to discern when the client is taking the bit in his teeth. And he needs to take charge of the situation right then.

The discontentment of the hunter I mentioned at the start of this chapter resulted from a situation where I simply failed to take charge. I was guiding a pair of clients in a two-on-one situation, and because they were friends who had booked the trip together, I thought it best to simply let them work out a certain matter between themselves. Hindsight showed that to be a mistake. I should have taken charge right from the start.

On the third day of their hunt, I took the pair into a high basin where I expected deer to be out feeding after a snow storm. After a good bit of hiking and glassing, I spotted a group of four bucks and got the hunters within 300 yards — as close as we could get in the open basin. Even at that the deer still sensed us. The hunters had to shoot more quickly, and at longer range, than would have been preferable.

There were two 5X5 bucks in the bunch, and after missing his first shot one of the hunters dropped the smaller of the five-points. His partner became a bit flustered as the other three bucks milled around and began to leave. He missed several more shots, and finally the bigger buck bolted into the timber and out of sight — or so it appeared.

The hunter fired several more shots at the smaller bucks as they bounded away. And when another big buck appeared even farther up the ridge he began shooting at it until I made him stop (It was far out of range.) It appeared he had missed his opportunity.

We climbed up the ridge to dress out the first hunter's buck, and when I reached it I noticed the bigger buck lying up the ridge just at the point where it had bolted from sight. It had been hit just as it bolted, but from our perspective below we hadn't been able to see it fall.

Unfortunately, the hunter who had shot the bigger buck had fallen behind as we climbed up to dress the deer. The problem began when his "friend," whose deer we had seen drop, immediately walked up to the bigger buck and said, "I got this one."

I honestly believe, looking back, that if I had said right then, "No, that's the one your partner shot," that the problem would have stopped right there. However, knowing that the clients were friends, and not yet realizing what the first hunter was really like, I decided at the time that it was best simply to be diplomatic and let the "friends" discuss it and settle the situation between themselves.

I backed up the second hunter when he pointed out to his partner that he had indeed shot the bigger buck. The tracks and the lay of the land proved it. I had watched the deer through binoculars zoomed in at 15x the whole time the hunters were shooting, so I knew which hunter had dropped which buck. However, it didn't help that the bigger one had dropped only after it bolted out of sight. That later compounded the problem.

The hunters agreed between themselves as to who would tag which buck, with each going to its rightful owner. We took photos, dressed them out, and went back to camp happy and satisfied — or so I thought.

The real problem arose the next day when the first hunter came with me to pack the bucks back to camp. When we skinned them out, we found that the bigger one had had its neck broken by a bullet. It should have simply dropped in its tracks, in plain view. If I hadn't seen it through 15x binoculars, I wouldn't have believed it myself. It could only have been hit just as it bolted.

The hunter with me then reasoned that if his partner had broken the buck's neck, we would have seen it drop. He began to theorize that he had actually shot the bigger one but didn't see it fall, then had shot the smaller of the two. By the time the trip was over he actually had himself convinced that he had shot two deer, his partner hadn't shot any, and that his tag belonged on the bigger buck.

As I mentioned before, the hunter's elk tag was already filled. So with little else to keep him occupied for the next five days he simply fretted and stewed. Slowly but steadily that hunter went from great satisfaction over the good hunting he had enjoyed to total discontentment

A guide must understand how to motivate and deal with each client according to his personality and abilities. That means "reading" each client to figure out just what makes him tick. The task is especially challenging in a two-on-one situation, where two different mentalities and abilities must be dealt with.

over not tagging the bigger of the bucks. And the whole situation could have been avoided if I had simply taken charge right at the start.

That isn't to say that you shouldn't be diplomatic. Always remember that bringing satisfied clients back as return business is one of your main duties as a guide. But often, simply establishing your control in a discreet but firm manner is a brand of diplomacy your client will appreciate. Because I failed to do that in the situation I just described, that client and I parted with a mutual disrespect for each other. Had I simply set things straight from the start, the client likely would have gone home satisfied.

There are also non-verbal ways of setting a client straight. I know of guides who have spent entire days leading a belligerent client through alder thickets, deadfall tangles or up steep mountains at an exhausting pace in order to remind that client who's who. Such tactics are a last resort and should be avoided if at all possible. But occasionally a guide does have to use such measures in order to remind a client who's in charge.

Once again, the best approach to any aspect of guiding is with a positive, confident attitude. That type of attitude is contagious and does more than anything else to maintain a good rapport with the client. Winning the client's confidence puts you in charge from the start. From there you can deal with each client according to his individual abilities and/or limitations.

Market competition makes for bold advertising claims, sensational cover blurbs, and dramatic photo layouts in the various hunting media. And while they're not necessarily unrealistic, only the attention-grabbing stories get published. All this makes for high expectations that a guide must do his best to live up to.

CHAPTER FIVE

MEETING THE CLIENT'S EXPECTATIONS

"You're going to have to guide the halt, the lame, and the blind for a while until you've gained some experience."

To a new guide I once worked with, those words stung like salt in a raw wound. Fresh out of guide school, he had champed at the bit for several weeks as he anticipated actually getting to guide hunters. The week before the season he had butterflies in his stomach. But when it finally got underway he found that not every hunter in camp was willing to trust him as a guide. The outfitter had to pull him aside and devastate him with that information.

The butterflies-in-the-stomach that the young guide had felt could easily have turned to sour grapes of disappointment. Just when he was gung-ho to call himself a guide, an older client virtually refused to be sent out with him. Having hunted with that outfitter a number of times before, the client had already gained a fair knowledge of the area and its game. He wasn't sure the new guide knew any more than he did.

Before the hunt was over, that guide did take the older hunter out, and the client ended up shooting a respectable three-point buck. Considering that the elderly client was developing cataracts, could do very little walking, and would probably not be physically able to make another hunt, his buck turned out to be the biggest trophy of the hunt, if not the season.

All's well that ends well, but that brand-new guide learned a painful but important lesson. It's not enough simply to go through a school, be trained by an outfitter, or even to be licensed as a guide, much less call yourself a guide. Clients have certain expectations, and every guide — especially an inexperienced one — will have to prove himself.

What You're Up Against

Ninety percent success rates on most hunts! Trophy Bulls! Trophy Bucks!

These eye-catching claims have no-doubt jumped at you from the ad pages of outdoor magazines.

Or you've probably read a hundred times how the huge bull elk came a' runnin', throwing sod, savaging trees and screeching like a wild banshee. By the time the hunter fired, he could see the red veins in the eyes of the rut-crazed bull and had to shoot in virtual self-defense. All he (or his guide) had to do was walk to a likely looking area, blow his Acme A-1 elk call, and watch the action unfold. It's that simple, right?

One hunting article I read a few years back was even accompanied by a photo caption that described the Bob Marshall Wilderness as an area where bull elk grow old and die without ever seeing a human. Having lived near it for enough of my life to be familiar with winter migration patterns, and having guided in it for a number of years, I know otherwise. But magazine editors and hunting clients like to think of it that way.

And of course there are the ever-common videos nowadays that show big buck after big buck within an hour- or half-hour-long time span. They hook the viewer with claims like "actual footage of trophy buck kills" or "experts demonstrate their secrets of success."

What the videos fail to mention, of course, is the hours and hours, or even days, weeks, and months that went into locating the game and filming the hunting scenes that the "experts" make look so easy. Many times most of the filming was done in national parks, wildlife refuges or even fenced-in private game preserves. (And recently, in separate incidents, two of the supposed experts who appear in videos were arrested for killing trophies illegally, one in Yellowstone Park.) But your clients don't know that.

Then there's the mystique, romance, or "Daniel Boone Syndrome" that goes with guides. Many clients (and perhaps many would-be guides as well) have a mental picture of a guide being so experienced and "woods wise" that he possesses some mystical power and uncanny hunting sense far greater than the average outdoorsman's ability.

Ideally, a guide should have that much experience and woods sense. However, given the increasing urbanization of our society, and the difficulty of making a long-term living as a guide, people with that much experience are becoming difficult to find and hire. A new guide may simply have to gain much of his experience on the job, especially if he's just out of guide school. But he'll still have the clients' high expectations to deal with, and rightly so.

What you're up against as a guide — especially as a new guide — is big dreams and expectations that have been planted and nurtured in the client's mind. Legend and mystique, photos and videos, books and magazines, and the client's own imagination all tend to inflate those expectations.

Every client you deal with will have already formed certain expectations regarding the outfitter, the area you'll take him into, the camp, the gear, the game or fish in the area, and even you as a guide. It's up to you to see that all those things measure up to the client's expectations — or else to change his expectations to fit the way things really are.

Not that the client's expectations are necessarily always unrealistic. Many of the photos and videos and stories the clients take in are true to life. The problem is that only the good ones get published. Hard work and monotony don't sell well, so what gets published is the easy-sounding success stories about big bucks, big bulls, big fish, and lots of them.

As one outdoor writer said, "No one wants to read about how you mucked around in the rain for two weeks and never saw any game." Even when a client knows better, the simple human tendency to dream creates high hopes that a guide must go up against — and, he hopes, live up to.

Creating the Right Expectations

Most outfitters make it a point in telephone conversations to tell clients or potential clients what to expect. And they virtually always mail out printed information containing a few photographs and describing the area the clients will hunt or fish.

Again, communication is crucial before and during the trip in order to establish the right expectations in the client's mind. Still, however, there will inevitably be those clients who show up with pre-conceived expectations based on prior experiences elsewhere or simply based on the magazine articles, photos and videos they've seen.

Just last fall I packed a disgruntled hunter out of camp at the end of a hunt. He complained because the area didn't match his expectations. Although the area was loaded with elk, the hunter complained that the outfitter hadn't described it well enough. It was thick with timber, deadfall and brush. The hunter expected the open, grassy parks he had seen in Colorado.

Unfortunately, preliminary communication sometimes fails because outfitters are afraid to be too realistic about game numbers and success ratios. They're afraid of losing clients. Some outfitters just plain lie. Others are truthful, but good business sense says that they should emphasize the more positive aspects of their operations rather than the hard realities.

Consequently a client, in his enthusiasm to pursue his dream, may fail to grasp the realities regarding game numbers, success rates, hunting conditions and factors beyond the guide's control. All too often they see what they want to see and hear what they want to hear.

The sad reality is that when preliminary communication fails, it falls to the guide himself to set the record straight without making the outfitter look bad. He has to set the tone early-on and establish the right expectations in the client. He must make sure that he does measure up to the client's expectations in terms of the effort he puts out to provide a top-notch experience. But he also has to make sure the client's expectations fall in line with reality.

Part of that can be accomplished verbally. More often though, the guide sets the tone by the competence, confidence, and conviction with which he goes about being a guide.

Whether he realizes it or not, a client hires you to do things your way, not his. (He may need to be reminded of that once in a while.) It's your job to know the territory and its critters and the best plan of attack. (Again, if that weren't the case, he wouldn't need to hire you.) Knowing what you're doing, then going about doing it with confidence and conviction will do more to set the tone and establish the right expectations than any amount of verbal wrangling will.

Image and Confidence

Again, a guide largely sets the stage by the way he comes across to the client. I know of an instance where a hunter arrived at his outfitter's home place and saw one of the guides outside loading up gear for the upcoming hunt. The client took one look at the guide and commented to the outfitter, "He looks like he could give you your money's worth."

Whatever the hunter saw in that particular guide, the guide had already established the hunter's confidence in him and set the tone for the hunt. He did it simply by looking and acting the part.

Clients won't come into camp knowing exactly how they expect a guide to look or act. But they do have a basic image in their minds that they expect each guide to live up to. Obviously that image will be different in a Maine whitetail camp than it will for a western horseback pack-in hunt or for a northern Canada fishing lodge. But no matter where you're working or what type of critter you're guiding for, every client will expect you to fit a certain image. A guide who makes a poor first impression by failing to look or act the part will have extra ground to make up in gaining the client's confidence.

As with anything, "looking the part" most often simply comes with experience. Until you've reached that point your best bet is to simply keep your mouth shut and your eyes open. Take a good look at some of the more seasoned locals. Not only will you learn how to look the part, you'll get an idea what clothing or gear works best in that region before you waste your money on something that doesn't. And you'll soon learn that it's easiest to look the part by *being the part*. You'll also learn how.

Unfortunately, I've seen prospective guides from other areas of the country come to the West and try to dress like what they think a cowboy, mountain man, or guide should look like. Too often their only basis for that image is what they've seen in Hollywood productions. The locals see right through them. Sadly, the clients usually do too.

Not that creating an "image" should be a guide's real goal or concern. A guide who's particularly image-conscious can often produce little more *than* an image. But to an extent the guiding business hinges on the "Daniel Boone Syndrome." Clients are paying, in part, for an image. It's part of the experience they're seeking, and again, poor first impressions mean playing catch-up. Conveying the right image wins their confidence from the start.

Confidence is also crucial to meeting a client's expectations. They want a guide who *knows* he will give them their money's worth. One who appears to lack confidence in his area's ability to produce game or fish — or worse, one who seems to lack confidence in his ability to find those critters — is a guide who will lose his client right from the start.

One evening a client and good friend of the outfitter I worked for pulled me aside and reminded me of that point. Not that I lacked confidence in my hunting or guiding ability. But perhaps I was a bit too much of a realist when it came to game numbers in our area, or the clients' chances of getting a shot. While I knew we were able to give them a good and enjoyable hunt, I was too realistic about clients' odds of success. Apparently that came across as a lack of confidence.

The outfitter's friend reminded me that evening that a guide must *exude* confidence. Every guide realizes that his country is tough to hunt, the clients have their limitations, and the game is widely dispersed. He realizes that only a certain percentage of clients will actually get game, or even a shot at it. But it's up to the outfitter to let the clients know about that end of things.

As a guide, it's up to you to be confident every time you take clients out that you're going to give them what they paid for. That's what keeps them confident, motivated, and in good spirits.

A new guide may feel like he's between a rock and a hard spot. He needs to come across as experienced and confident, but he lacks the experience that produces confidence and wins the client's trust. That's just something every new guide has to deal with. Everyone has to start somewhere. He still must exude confidence.

Again, it's not that trying to create an image should be your goal in and of itself. Any client will see right through that false "veneer" when the moment of truth comes. But gaining experience — and learning all you can from those who already have it — will automatically create the image and confidence that measure up to the clients' expectations. And more importantly, those qualities will make the clients' expectations fit the guide.

Dealing With Pressure

When a client is laying out anywhere from several hundred to several thousand dollars for an outfitted and guided hunting or fishing trip, there will always be pressure to produce. That pressure may come from the client, the outfitter, or from you yourself as a guide.

The pressure may be to produce game, or it may be to produce something else the client believes he is paying for. But in some form or to some extent, pressure will always be there. The question is not whether you will feel pressure to produce as a guide, but rather how you will deal with it.

You could take an apathetic approach and simply not care whether the client is satisfied or not. But chances are that would ruin the experience for that client — which in turn would result in even more pressure and problems for you. Or you could go to the other extreme and constantly worry and fret about whether your client fills his tags, catches his limit, etc. That would ruin the whole guiding experience for you.

Taking a balanced approach is the only way a guide can deal with pressure responsibly and still enjoy a guiding career the way it ought to be enjoyed. It's important to take guiding seriously and do your best for the client. But once you've done that it's pointless to put pressure on yourself over what you can't control.

I guided several seasons for an outfitter who frequently said, "We don't worry about what we can't do nothin' about." That approach let him fully enjoy providing good experiences for clients by putting his energy into the things he *could* do something about.

The easiest way to avoid pressure as a guide is to do your best in the things you *can* control. Something else I learned from the same outfitter is that most successful outfitters are noted for having comfortable, well kept camps, using reliable stock and equipment, and serving excellent food. Those are things they can do something about.

For a guide, having an upbeat, positive attitude, putting out an honest daylight-to-dark effort, and treating your clients the best you know how are things you *can* do something about. It's up to the outfitter to tell clients what their odds of success are and what to expect. It's up to the client to make adequate mental and physical preparation. Past that, if you've done your best, the rest is beyond your control, so don't worry about it and don't apologize when the clients don't get the game they think they've paid for. As another top-notch outfitter says, "I don't sell elk; I sell hunts."

I've made the mistake at times of feeling guilty or sorry if a hunting client didn't get game, because I knew how much money he had laid out in order to make the trip. Like many clients, I allowed my focus to fall only on getting game, even though I knew better, and it took the enjoyment out of the job for me.

In most of those cases, the clients were perfectly satisfied anyway. Sure, they were sorry they didn't score. But they knew I'd done my best and that they had had a good hunt. When the guide puts that kind of pressure on himself, he's making a big mistake.

Most clients fall into the category I just described. They're sorry if they don't get what they're hunting or fishing for, but they know success is never guaranteed. They're happy if you did your best and gave them a good trip.

The rest usually fall into one of two categories. Some will never be happy, no matter what you do for them. Like the hunter I described at the start of Chapter Four, even though they've had a good experience, gotten top-notch service, and gotten the game they came for, they'll still find things to complain about. Don't take their complaints overly seriously. Let them be miserable if they choose to, but don't let them make you miserable.

The others will always be easy to please, because they don't feel they have to prove anything to themselves or anyone else. They're just there to enjoy life. Those are the ones who make guiding a pleasure, because they appreciate all that they experience and all you do for them. They feel no pressure to accomplish anything except what falls their way, and they put no such pressure on you. Don't expect every client to be like that, but relish working with the few who are.

I worked for a very successful outfitter who said that early in his career he let it bother him when clients didn't get their game. But he finally came to the conclusion that if he stopped outfitting those clients, someone else would just come in and do it in his place. He realized that he might as well be the one doing the outfitting, and he might as well enjoy it. He no longer let that pressure bother him. The same should be true for guides.

Again, confidence comes into play when dealing with pressure. A confident, positive attitude in a guide sets the stage early-on. And it carries through when bad circumstances prevail. When the outfitter has done his part to let the client know what to expect, and you as a guide have done your best — when you have controlled the things you're able to control — then you can be confident that sooner or later the rest will fall into place. And if it doesn't, that's just a part of hunting or fishing we all have to live with. Your positive, confident approach to that reality will steer the client toward realistic expectations.

CHAPTER SIX

DEALING WITH THE OUTFITTER

Maybe trouble had been brewing all season. Maybe it had just flared up. Perhaps the guides should have known what they were getting into ahead of time, and maybe they should have stuck it out. But when the crew packed out from setting up a hunting camp, one of the guides simply tied up his packstring and left. A short time later, after setting up a spike camp, another guide did the same thing.

Perhaps the problem was the outfitter's fault, maybe it was the guides' fault, maybe both were to blame. I don't know the details. But the outfitter came out short of help when he needed it most. He ended up having to hire whatever guides he could pick up out of a local bar.

The guides lost out on the season's pay and experience as well as any chance of a good recommendation. They obviously had a problem in their dealings with the outfitter, and both the outfitter and the guides came out losers.

All too often both outfitters and guides give themselves needless headaches. They lose out on good jobs, good help, and a season's worth of enjoyable experiences simply because they fail to deal sensibly or appropriately with each other. Short tempers, stubbornness, trouble swallowing pride, poor communication, or a simple lack of dependability on the part of one or both is usually at the root of the problem. The sad part is that with just a little common sense and self-discipline most of the problems could be avoided. Here's a look at it from the guide's perspective.

Landing the Job
"Good. I'll hire you. How soon can you be here?"

Which guide would you hire if you were a client? That's what an outfitter looks for. Obviously, a change in clothing won't change your ability as a guide, but it does change the way you come across. Your appearance reflects your professionalism and your attitude toward serving clients. A "duded-up" guide is easy to see through, just as a poor appearance reflects apathy.

Those words from an outfitter wrapped up a very brief conversation with a young guide who was looking for work. The conversation was too brief, in fact. The outfitter wanted to hire the guide sight-unseen over the phone with no references and no more than a few words to judge by. Wisely, the guide sensed that an outfitter so eager to hire must be an outfitter who was desperate. And he must have been desperate for a reason.

The young man had gone through an outfitter's school the previous year and had been hired as a guide by that same outfitter. He had been caught in some shady dealings on the outfitter's part, but the two had patched up their differences. The following year that outfitter was too short on clients to be able to hire the young guide back. However, in an effort to place his graduate in a job elsewhere he put him in touch with an outfitter from another state who had called in search of qualified help. That was the outfitter who seemed too eager to hire.

A few days later, that same guide was talking to a friend who ran an archery shop and had hunted with an outfitter the previous fall. His friend spoke highly of the outfitter and suggested asking him for a job. It turned out that the outfitter did need help, but not so desperately that he was eager to hire just anyone. After each did a bit of checking on the other, both outfitter and guide were satisfied that their employment relationship would work out well. They've since had two good seasons working together.

There's no guarantee that even a well done background check will assure a perfect match-up between outfitter and guide. But it's a good place to start. When you're eager to get into a guiding career, it's tempting to jump at the first job possibility that comes your way. However, make sure you find out as much as possible beforehand and know what you're getting into. Once you've committed on a job, you're committed for the entire season. There's very rarely, if ever, any excuse for quitting before the season is out.

It's best to see an operation first-hand before going to work for it. For three seasons I worked with a guide who had first been a client with the outfitter I was working for. He established such a rapport with the crew and showed such an interest in the operation that when the outfitter was in need of a guide, that client was his first choice to hire.

Obviously that's an ideal situation. It's rarely possible to look over and compare various outfits, much less hunt with them before hiring on. However, it's best to talk extensively with an outfitter, take a good look at his brochures, and ask plenty of questions before committing to a job.

For someone who wants to be a guide but has had no real exposure to the outfitting industry, the biggest problem may be that of not knowing what questions to ask. Even if you've gone through a guide school and are being placed on a job, it's still difficult to know what to ask before committing.

My own first-job interview was much along those lines. I had no real idea what I should iron out verbally before taking the job, and but for the grace of God I might well have ended up with an outfit where I didn't belong. Fortunately, the outfitter running the school was well acquainted with the one he placed me with, so he knew I'd be with a reputable outfit. That first job lasted five good seasons, but not everyone has been so fortunate.

Even a school can rarely guarantee the outfitter they're placing you with, so it's important to ask the right questions before hiring on. If you're at a loss as to just how to approach a job interview, here are suggestions from other guides and outfitters themselves:

1) To begin with, *Sell Yourself!* Do it with HONESTY and MODESTY, but also with CONFIDENCE. This comes from a guide-school instructor, but I've given similar advice myself. As intimidating as any job interview may be — especially when trying to land your first guiding job — it's important that you be confident in yourself.

No one expects you to be an old hand at guiding if that's not what you are. But clients *don't* want a guide who lacks confidence in himself, so no outfitter will want one either. Remember, the worst that can happen is the outfitter might say he can't use you, and you'll simply need to try again elsewhere.

Again, though, remember honesty and modesty. I once advised a would-be guide to show confidence when approaching my employer about a job. When asked about his hunting experience he said yes, he had killed a couple of elk. When asked if he had experience with horses and packing, he said, "Oh, anybody can do that!" So much for modesty.

Maybe the kid misunderstood my suggestion regarding confidence, or maybe he would have responded that way anyhow. Either way he didn't get the job. As for honesty, anything but the truth will soon come back to haunt you. Being honest with yourself as well as the outfitter about your inexperience doesn't mean lacking confidence in yourself. Be honest but *sell yourself!*

2) *Look the part!* The way you dress won't affect your ability as a

potential guide, but it does reflect your professionalism and your attitude toward the job. Clients expect a guide to fit a certain image, so outfitters want to hire guides who look the part. It's pretty hard to go wrong looking at least somewhat "western," no matter where you're asking for the job. Just make sure it's an honest-to-goodness western, and not a Nashville or Hollywood version, as I've already discussed. But if you're talking to the outfitter in person, look the part when you look for a job.

3) Get a good *Job Description*. That is, get an all-encompassing run-down of what's expected of you. Find out what you'll be doing, and for how long (length of the season). Find out how many hours you'll be expected to work each day, how many days you're expected to work each week, and how many you're *likely* to work. Although there is rarely such a thing as a "typical" work week in the outfitting business, ask for a rough idea of what a given week might be like during each phase of the season (fishing, packing, hunting, etc.).

It's important to find out ahead of time just what to expect and what's expected of you. As one outfitter put it, "A lot of guys think they're just going to ride a white horse and kill six-point bulls all the time." They find out the hard way there's a lot more to guiding than that.

4) Look through the outfitter's brochure so you know what he's selling his clients and what they expect of him. Knowing that will give you a better idea of what the clients (and outfitter) expect of you.

5) Find out what you can expect of the outfitter, and what you *should* expect of him.

• First, is he licensed? Don't take this for granted. All too often outfitters operate illegally, without the required state license or permits from public land-use agencies. I know a guide who nearly got burned by such an outfitter this past year. A number of that outfitter's guide-school students did get taken, simply because they didn't make sure he was properly licensed. Be especially careful of outfitters who want to be paid in cash by their clients or students, or who want to pay you in cash.

• Is he insured? Most states, if not all, require outfitters to carry at least a certain amount of liability insurance as well as pay Worker's Compensation Insurance on their employees. Make sure the outfitter complies with state requirements in that regard, and don't take a job where you won't be covered at least by Worker's Comp. Guiding isn't necessarily a hazardous occupation, but it places you in plenty of situations where you have opportunities to get injured — and possibly end up unable to work.

• What kinds of equipment does he use? One outfitter mentioned an acquaintance who hauls his stock in a 25-year-old 48-foot semi and expects his guides to be able to drive it. Even his own two-ton stock truck is more than some guides might be able to handle, or are comfortable handling.

• Talk to some of his employees, if you can, and find out from them what he's like to work for. If wages include room and board, ask if he feeds adequately and if the living quarters are serviceable. Find out how long his employees have been around, if they come back to work year after year. Other factors may be involved, but if an outfitter's employees don't come back from one season to the next, it may be that he pays poorly or is simply unpleasant to work for.

6) Wait until the end of the conversation to discuss wages. Rushing into questions about money can give the impression of being in this only for yourself and for what you can get out of it. That doesn't mean you shouldn't discuss wages at all, however. Some outfitters may hire you for just as little as you're willing to settle for, and some may leave the matter open, then pay you less than what you expected. You don't have to nail it down during your first conversation, but agree on a wage before you take a job.

It's best to know ahead of time what wage you'll need in order to get by, and a rough minimum you're willing to work for. That way you won't have to hem and haw when the outfitter makes an offer. Figure up your monthly living expenses, plus any expenses you anticipate for gear or special clothing, and in your mind set a bottom-line figure you can settle for.

Know what your time and sweat are worth to you, but also take into account that what you'll experience as a guide is worth quite a bit too when weighed against whatever sacrifices, financial or otherwise, that way of life requires. Check around and have a rough idea what guides with your level of experience are being paid in the area. Then make sure you can get by on that. If the outfitter offers you more, great. If not, you may have to look elsewhere or get your necessities whittled down to where you're willing and able to live on what's being offered.

Communication

Communication is just as crucial between the guide and the outfitter as it is between the guide and his client. And perhaps knowing what each one expects of the other is the most crucial area of all.

Probably the only real negative experience I've had with an outfitter resulted from a lack of communication. More specifically, it stemmed from failure to clear up our expectations of each other. The outfitter neglected to tell me just what he expected of me, and I neglected to ask him when I hired on. Having already had a number of years' experience, I assumed I knew what the outfitter wanted from me, and he assumed the same.

As the summer season wore on and hunting season approached, that outfitter and I began to find that our expectations of each other didn't match up. But all along he had neglected to tell me what he wanted from me until the situation finally came to a head. I still consider that outfitter a friend, but the following year I went elsewhere and had a great season with another outfit. The whole situation could have been avoided with just a bit of communication on the part of the outfitter or me as a guide.

Communication is crucial in every aspect of a guide's work, and he needs to maintain a good rapport with the rest of the crew and especially the outfitter. An outfitter must often delegate jobs to various guides, and he can't always know himself if one of the vehicles needs repairs or a saddle needs fixed or a mule is pulling up lame. Without guides keeping him well informed, the outfitter can't plan work schedules and stock rotations or the use of various vehicles and equipment effectively.

Occasionally two members of the crew just won't mix, and it's not at all uncommon for a guide to find he just doesn't match up well with the client he's been paired up with. But all too often these minor problems become major problems simply because guides don't let the outfitter know they exist. Instead they grouse and complain among themselves and never bother to talk to the person who can actually do something about it. Again, communication is always crucial in dealing with the outfitter you work for.

Coachability/Versatility

I once heard an outfitter complain that frequently when he hired new guides, within a few weeks they were trying to tell him how to run his outfit — or at best they were trying to do things their own way. One thing every guide needs to learn, and to remember throughout his career, is that every operation is unique. Every outfitter has his own way of doing things, and he does them that way for a reason. It's important that his guides learn to do things his way.

To be worth his salt, a guide must be coachable. Any outfitter who has his operation organized well enough to be successful will have most of it reduced to a system that works efficiently for him. His crew will fold all their mantie tarps the same way, coil all their pack ropes the same way, tie up all the sling ropes on their pack saddles the same way, tie off all their latigos the same way, stack all their saddles and pads the same way, etc. The whole operation runs much more smoothly when everyone follows the same system.

Any guide who is unwilling or unable to learn things the outfitter's way will be a liability to the outfitter and the crew. Sooner or later he'll find himself in a jackpot, needing to pull a pack or a saddle loose in a hurry, and he'll lose time because they're not tied off his way. Or worse, another crew member will be in a jam and lose crucial time, risking injury to himself or his stock — simply because someone else did things his own way rather than by the outfitter's system.

Even just when unloading the pack strings at the end of a long day, or when getting packed up in the morning, valuable time is lost when one of the crew has to break his routine because someone insisted on doing things his own way.

Granted, the fact that an outfitter has his own way of doing things doesn't mean his way is always right. But again, he's the one calling the shots. As one outfitter told me, "Our way isn't necessarily always the best, but it's what works for us."

If you have a better idea, it doesn't hurt to suggest it to the outfitter in a diplomatic way. But don't insist on doing things your way. If you're not willing to be coachable and versatile and learn to do things his way, you shouldn't hire on with an outfitter in the first place.

Flexibility

One of the most frequent complaints I've heard among guides is that plans are constantly changing. It's been that way in almost every outfit I've worked for.

Some outfitters are better planners than others, and the smaller the operation, the easier it is to set a plan and stick with it. However, circumstances beyond anyone's control can be a big factor in any outfitter's business, and they seem to crop up at the most inopportune times.

Whether it's horses getting loose in the night, vehicles breaking down, bad storms blowing in, accidents and injuries to other members of the crew, or simply the boss-man changing his mind, any number of factors will make the best-laid plans subject to change without notice. A guide who can't flex and adapt with the circumstances while maintaining a good attitude is, again, a liability rather than an asset to the outfitter and crew. Roll with the punches.

Dependability

His patience exhausted, an irate outfitter pounded loudly on the door of his guide's trailer house. It was already 6:00 a.m. The horses were long-since loaded in the stock truck, breakfast was over, and the hunters and guides should have left for the trailhead an hour ago.

Finally, after continued loud knocking, the guide's girlfriend answered the door. "Oh, he's not working for you anymore," she replied when the outfitter asked gruffly why his employee had failed to show up. "We're going to Coeur d'Alene tomorrow and getting married."

It was bad enough that the guide hadn't bothered telling the outfitter he wasn't coming to work. But worse, he had quit cold turkey in the middle of hunting season. The outfitter had made a commitment to his

An outfitter's livelihood rides on his guides' dependability. He counts on each guide to stick out the season. He trusts them with his stock, equipment and clients. He needs guides who do a job well without supervision no matter what the conditions.

clients, and they had already arrived. He could no longer keep that commitment. It was too late to find another guide.

The choice to work as a guide involves a commitment. It's not merely a job that one can walk away from and start up somewhere else anytime he chooses. When a guide hires on with an outfit, he does it with the understanding that, barring unforseen events beyond his or the outfitter's control, he's on for the whole season.

The outfitting industry is built largely on commitment and dependability. Because it's mainly seasonal, the outfitter must be able to do most of his booking months in advance, and then hire the crew needed to service his clients. When he books a pack trip or hunting or fishing trip, he and the client sign a contract, and his ability to fulfill that contract often depends on the reliability of his hired help. He can't just hire another qualified guide anytime one walks out on him. So hiring on as a guide means committing for the entire season and sticking it out come what may.

Granted, not every outfitter deserves to have guides that stick out the season with him. Often those who complain most about undependable guides are those who treat their guides the poorest. I've known of instances where an outfitter wouldn't pay his guides what he said he would, or had such a negative temperament he was unbearable to work for, or fed so poorly that both guides and clients had to kill grouse to eat while out hunting elk. However, again that gets back to what you as a guide should find out about an outfit before hiring on. Once you've committed for the season as a guide, only the worst offense on the part of an outfitter would justify your quitting him before the season's out.

Naturally, dependability applies to more than just sticking out the season. A guide must be dependable in every task he performs every day of the year. If you're haphazard and careless in the work you do now, or you're not punctual and reliable in your everyday commitments, then the life of a guide is not for you. The demands of a guide's job require someone who can be depended on in all circumstances.

Responsibility

To an extent, responsibility falls within the scope of dependability, but it goes even a step further. Like the cream that rises to the top of fresh milk, the guides who really rise to the top are those who can be relied upon to step forward and take responsibility. They go beyond just sticking around through the course of a season and doing what they're instructed to do. A guide who truly becomes valuable to an outfitter is one who can see for himself what needs to be done and then takes responsibility and initiative beyond just what he's told to do.

To be an asset to his employer (and the clients he ultimately serves) a guide needs to be someone the outfitter can delegate to. Not just in the sense of working without supervision, but one who can take charge of a crew and see that things get done the way the outfitter needs them done. The guide who frees his employer up from tending to menial chores and supervisory headaches is the one who will be asked to return each year. That's also the guide who will see his wages increase season after season.

Taking Over the Outfit

At first an outfitter might cringe at this notion, but in reality it's to his advantage. Every guide's goal should be to progress to the point where he knows enough and is reliable enough that he could take over his employer's operation. The more of that operation a guide can run, the fewer headaches the outfitter has to deal with.

There's an added bonus here too. Eventually, as the years go by, every outfitter wears down and wants to sell out and retire. For a guide who wants to run his own outfitting business — and for an outfitter who wants to sell out — what better option is there than a guide who already knows the business from the inside out?

Camp can be bleak and lonesome for a guide who is homesick or longs for the glitter of city lights. Hard to imagine, but some guides want out of the backcountry almost as soon as they get in. (Photo courtesy Wildlife Adventures, Inc.)

CHAPTER SEVEN

COMMON GUIDE PROBLEMS

"An outfitter is only as good as his worst guide."

More than one outfitter has wisely realized and stated that fact.

An outfitter can provide all the best stock and equipment, set up comfortable, deluxe camps, and serve twice as much top-notch cooking as his clients (and crew) could ever eat. He could take those clients into the most rugged, majestic and remote country they could ever imagine, and he could see that they get into parts of that country that are loaded with fish or game.

However, if that outfitter's guides fail to do their part, or if they somehow offend or disillusion his guests, those same clients will find another outfitter. Which in turn means less business for the outfitter and lower wages — or possibly even unemployment — for the problem guide.

A guide may be the best hunter in his own neck of the woods, or the best at getting his clients into fish, etc., but he must realize that public relations is at least half his job. As stated earlier in the book, most outfitters would rather have a guide who's a mediocre hunter but is reliable and good with clients. A guide who's great at finding game but can't be counted on by the outfitter, or who leaves a bad taste in clients' mouths, will lose more business than he brings back.

Guide problems don't always necessarily have to do with the way a guide deals directly with the client. A number of personal problems commonly show up amongst guides, but unfortunately they affect the outfitter and clients too. Most could be easily cured, or better yet avoided in the first place. This chapter deals with a number of those problems and how to steer clear of them.

Loneliness, Homesickness

Believe it or not, this occasionally is a problem for some guides. I've particularly seen it in would-be guides who have come from some other part of the country, have never been away from home much before, and show up at a guide school with visions of grandeur, thinking they'll live out their glamorous dream. They would never have imagined it would happen to them, but they find themselves feeling so alone in their strange new surroundings that they pack up and head home.

As often as not, those who are so inclined will quit and go home before they've even gotten a good taste of the situation or given themselves time to get used to it. However, I recently heard of a student who had stuck it out and graduated from a guide school, but then got so homesick he ended up quitting and going back home in the middle of the hunting season. He left the outfitter in a lurch.

You may find it hard to imagine yourself having such problems. But be aware that such problems do arise — before you commit yourself to a guide school. And especially think it over before committing to a job. An outfitter must be able to count on you for the entire season.

A smaller, but similar and more common problem is that of guides not wanting to spend long periods of time in the backcountry. They want to live the life of a guide, but they miss the lights of the city. Such guides become a nuisance to the outfitter when they constantly pester him for a chance to get down to the dance halls and honky-tonks or whatever other attractions they find in the cities.

Drinking

One of the better guides I know stops all drinking as soon as hunting camp is being set up. He won't drink again until the season is over. He's seen the problems that arise with guides who get into booze. For example, not getting out of bed when they should, not getting their work done or doing it poorly, or not serving the client the way they would want to be served if they were in his boots.

Even outfitters themselves have been ruined by foolishly dipping into the sauce. As hunting consultant Jack Atcheson has written, "Alcohol, outfitting and divorce are often synonymous."

I heard of one unfortunate client who arrived for a pack-in hunting trip and was picked up at the airport by a half-pickled guide. When they arrived at the trailhead, the outfitter was also drunk. Before long, the outfitter and his guide had disagreed over something and had gotten into

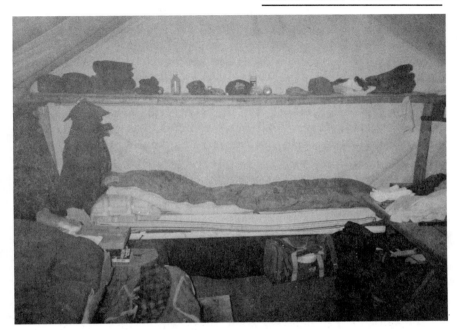

Guides' quarters. Not always fancy, but appealing at times. Leaving a warm, comfortable sleeping bag and the heat of the wood stove for a cold saddle and a long, hard day takes motivation on the guide's part. As the season takes its toll, motivation can dwindle — a problem for many guides. (Photo courtesy Scott Boulanger)

a fight. They began wrestling and rolling around on the ground trying to get the best of each other. Before long the outfitter's wife joined the fray, whacking the guide across the head with a frying pan.

The whole affair may sound a bit comical at first, but it won't when you're the one responsible for such a debacle (or a worse one) simply because you didn't say "No" to booze. I don't know if that client stuck around for the duration of the hunt, or if he decided better of it after what he'd just seen. He would have been well justified in simply packing up, leaving, and suing the outfitter for a refund. Drunken guides can be a real liability to clients, outfitters, and ultimately themselves.

Even when guides don't become so out-and-out drunk that they can't do their jobs, their effectiveness suffers due to other side-effects of even moderate drinking. Tempers wear thin; judgement grows poor; stock, fellow crew members, and even clients get mistreated; motivation diminishes; quality of work drops off. Ultimately the whole operation and everyone involved begins to suffer, whether they themselves have done any drinking or not.

Most outfitters allow alcohol in their camps. They leave the choice as to whether to drink, and how much, to the guests and the guides themselves. For some clients, unfortunately, that's the whole point of their trip.

Some outfitters even bring their own supply of booze. But they still expect the guides to be up and ready to go well before daylight every morning. Those concerned about success rates expect the guests to be able to get up and go each morning as well. The wise ones, however, won't let the clients go near their rifles, much less go out and hunt, with so much as the smell of alcohol on their breath.

Strangely enough, the choice not to drink can nearly cause a guide problems as well. Ironically, the guide who normally quit drinking when hunting camp went up was the one who asked me, "You're not going to have one glass of beer — even half a glass — to celebrate with us?" We had just come off a very successful hunt. I drank a Coke while they drank beer, and we had just as much fun as if I'd been drinking alcohol. But some clients (and guides) have difficulty comprehending that.

For whatever reason, people often seem to attach some symbolic "fellowship" or "camaraderie" significance to the act of imbibing alcohol together. Many seem to think they can't be having fun if there's no alcohol in what they're drinking — or in what you're drinking with them. It should make no difference whether you're drinking pop, coffee, water, lemonade, or whatever else with them. The point should be enjoying the camp camaraderie, not whether there's alcohol in what you drink.

If, like me, you don't drink at all and you simply say so, clients will accept that — especially if you prove yourself as a guide. It's foolish to equate masculinity or your competence as a guide with drinking booze, but most folks need to be reminded of that. And once you show your savvy as a guide (which you'll do better without being influenced by booze) most clients will respect that.

Clients and other guides will frequently want you to drink with them so they can feel like they're "having one with the boys." Just remember, any alcohol you drink affects you as a guide, it affects the client, and it affects everyone else in camp — never in a positive way. My own personal advice is, "Don't drink. Period." No one's enjoyment has to depend on booze, and too many problems result from drinking.

Motivation

Usually, as the opening of the season draws near, most hunting or fishing guides are champing at the bit. However, after a few days of getting up early, coming back late, going hard all day and getting few hours of sleep, some guides' enthusiasm starts to wane. By the time the season is nearing its end, virtually all guides are worn down and looking forward to some time off.

Lack of motivation can be a result of different factors for different guides. In some cases it's simply a built-in character flaw. But in many cases it's due to the wear-and-tear, the demands and grind of the guide's job throughout the season.

Every week or ten days, a fresh batch of clients comes in all rested, pumped full of adrenaline, charged with anticipation and ready to go. For the first part of the season, the guide is charged up too. However, as time goes along, the guide may have had his fill of the country, the clients, and the hunting or fishing they came for. The clients are motivated, the guide isn't, and problems can soon arise.

If the hunting or fishing have been especially poor, guiding can become monotonous. When the clients are difficult to please or are simply inept and incompetent, guides soon tire of dealing with them and baby-sitting them. As the physical demands of the job take their toll, tiredness sets in and ambition dwindles.

For a guide who's in it only for himself, there will be little motivation left. The paycheck at the end of the month may be his only incentive at that point. It's crucial that a guide remember how much each client has invested in his trip financially, physically and emotionally. (It may be that client's once-in-a-lifetime dream.) It's also crucial that he remember how extensively the outfitter's entire livelihood rests on every aspect of each guide's performance.

Every guide has to keep himself motivated to honor his commitment to the outfitter and the client. Lack of motivation spells trouble.

Personal Cleanliness

When they were boys, a lot of men probably got tired of hearing the old adage, "Cleanliness is next to godliness." (I don't know where it originated, but it's not in the Bible.) By the time they had grown up, however, a lot of those same men seem to have decided that "dirtiness is next to manliness."

Sometimes guides get the mistaken notion that the more they cuss and chew and stink and look grimy, the better guide they are. They seem to think that the dirtier they are in their personal habits, the better they'll fit the guide's image and impress the client. Or some are just so ignorant they simply don't realize how dirty they are, or that it offends those around them. Neither notion could be further from the truth.

Living and working conditions for a guide are such that being dirty, to an extent, simply goes with the job. You don't have to fit an image by trying to stay dirty. That part will take care of itself. Trying to stay clean is the hard part, and it's more important than many guides realize. Again, public relations is at least half of a guide's job.

For backcountry hunts, most outfitters set up at least a makeshift shower arrangement in a tent with a wood stove. Those who don't will have some arrangement by which a guide can take a sponge bath a time or two during the course of a hunt. And even if they don't get you out of the backcountry fairly often, they'll usually arrange to get your laundry done. The very least a guide can do is wash his hands before

Just a few minutes with these simple hygiene items does wonders. And there's always cold running water. If the weather's at all conducive, there's nothing more exhilarating or rejuvenating than a dip in a mountain stream.

every meal — before handling food or dishes in the cook tent.

The clients will understand that baths or showers in the backcountry are often few and far between. They may tolerate a little trail dust and hay chaff on a guide's clothes, or even a few days' sweat and grime. But when you neglect to change clothes occasionally and smell so bad your client can't stand to be near you, he may ask to be paired with another guide. And when you handle his food or dishes without washing your hands — especially after gutting elk or brushing horses or using the latrine — that client will be sure to let the outfitter know that you're the reason he'll be hunting elsewhere next year.

Ethics

I once heard a game warden tell of a guide whose elk hunting client illegally shot a moose. The guide immediately informed the outfitter of the problem. After two weeks, the outfitter finally got around to reporting the kill to authorities.

It could be that the outfitter intended all along to report the violation but just couldn't get out of the backcountry for two weeks. But he may have held off reporting it in hopes of finding some way to just cover it up and get by with it. Technically, the game warden couldn't prosecute the outfitter, because he did eventually report the illegal kill. However, after that the authorities always had that nagging doubt as to how honest the outfitter was.

The guide, on the other hand, had done the right thing and cleared his name by reporting the offense immediately. The authorities, probably, would always regard him as someone they could trust because he had done what was ethically right.

The ethics relating to various aspects of the guiding profession run a wide gamut. They involve everything from game laws and National Forest regulations to how humanely you treat your livestock. They range from the way you deal with clients to how you impact natural resources. Quite often, a guide's ethics involve hunting or fishing tactics and practices. And authorities usually learn who they need to keep an eye on and who they can trust.

A guide's approach to ethics is often a reflection on the outfitter he's working for. A shoddy or shady outfitter will likely hire guides of the same character; a top-notch outfitter will be ethical and will expect the same from his guides. It's always crucial that a guide keep his practices above-board and ethical. An outfitter's entire business investment and livelihood can easily hinge on those ethics.

A practice that is becoming commonplace, and which could pose problems for uninitiated guides, is that of the U.S. Fish & Wildlife Service or various state game agencies "planting" officers who pose as clients in hunting camps. These "plants" will offer guides and outfitters money to let them take extra game, protected species, or trophy animals they don't have permits for. That's fine as long as it's used to pin the goods on known offenders.

However, I've also heard of such officers deliberately creating or committing an offense by killing more than their limit or taking game without a permit. (The ethics of such practices is something these agencies have to consider.) Planted agents will sometimes do this just to see if the guide or outfitter will handle the situation according to law.

Make sure your client, and the outfitter, know right from the start where you stand in case of violations, and don't waffle when it comes to reporting them. A sympathetic guide who thinks he's simply trying to cover for a client's mistake may find himself facing huge state or federal fines, plus loss of his guide's license. And again, he also risks jeopardizing the outfitter's livelihood.

Most ethical dilemmas come in areas not specifically covered by law. (The laws are black and white.) The problem with a guide making poor ethical choices, whether covered by law or not, is that he does more than just put himself and his employer at risk.

When a guide furthers his own success by questionable means, he ends up cheating those outfitters and guides who operate honestly and ethically. And he gives the entire industry a bad reputation. One client who had been burned by a shady outfitter said he would never return to that outfitter's state. Every outfitter in the state suffered for one outfitter or guide's poor ethics.

All too often poor ethical practices are fostered by the outfitter himself in a short-sighted effort to build his success rates and bookings. However, that's not always the case, and it's never an excuse. A guide ultimately has to make his own decisions and stand on his own two feet. If you can't agree with an outfitter's ethics, you shouldn't work for him. Ultimately, you may even be put in a position of having to report an unethical operation to the appropriate authorities.

Girlfriends/Marriage

A girlfriend or a wife is a great thing, but they rarely mix well with a guiding career. Granted, it's very difficult for an outfitter to succeed in the business without having a strong, dedicated wife teamed up with him. And it's tough to find a strong, dedicated marriage partner without doing some dating first. But a guide with a wife or serious girlfriend rarely remains a guide for very long. Worse, he often gets into conflicts, or creates conflicts for the outfitter and crew, while he still remains a guide.

When a guide has a wife, he usually ends up neglecting his work or neglecting his wife, or neglecting both to some extent. Usually he can't support a wife adequately. And when a young guide has a girlfriend, he usually won't have the maturity to keep his mind off her and keep his focus on his work. (Don't think it can't happen to *you*.)

Plenty of husband/wife teams work well together running camps for outfitters. Wives usually work as camp cooks and bookkeepers, but they sometimes work right alongside their husbands guiding clients or handling stock. The problem is that guiding is most often seasonal, so if they don't own the outfit it's tough for married couples to live off guides' wages.

When a guide's spouse does not work alongside him in the business, usually one of two things will occur. Either he will get spread too thin, torn between his commitment to the outfitter and his commitment to his wife, or else his wife will get just plain lonesome with her husband gone all the time.

In the first case both commitments suffer, neither getting its just due. In the second case, the guide usually finds another career so he can be with his wife and support her properly. In most cases, both results take place, in that order.

With unmarried guides, girlfriends can be an equally large problem. As long as the guide is in the backcountry and his girlfriend is in town, things usually work out okay. But when guiding and girlfriends mix, that's when trouble starts.

No doubt the most common problem with guides having girlfriends is, again, the guides forget to keep their minds on their responsibilities. That's no new revelation. Every young man faces that problem whether he's a guide or not. But when guides start bringing their girlfriends into camp, the potential for problems really increases.

No matter how focused a guide tries to stay, when his girlfriend (or wife) is in camp, inevitably he'll be putting attention and effort toward her that he should be putting toward clients. Even if he's not totally caught up in a romantic swoon, he'll still be making sure she's warm enough, dry enough, comfortable enough, etc., rather than making sure the clients, stock, and chores are tended to.

All too often guides want to sleep with their girlfriends, or want their girlfriends to sleep with them, and that's where real trouble can start. Either they have to set up extra sleeping accommodations, or worse, they want to bring their girlfriends in the guides' quarters. Then even more of their attention goes toward their girlfriends than toward their work. The other guides' privacy is imposed on, and clients or co-workers may be offended by the lack of morals.

Don't take me wrong. Girlfriends and marriage are natural and very good in their rightful place. I'm not knocking either of them. In fact, I recommend both. I've enjoyed several good years of marriage myself and am glad I got married. I have a good wife who knew going into marriage what she was getting into. I enjoyed three years of guiding even after getting married — more than most married guides do.

Still, I found that if I'd been single during those years I could have done more for the outfitters I worked with. And after three years, my wife reluctantly admitted that she was just plain lonesome. For six months out of the year I was gone for eight or ten days at a time with only a day at home between trips. She had tried to fill up the emptiness, but nothing took the place of a husband being at home for her.

A lot of guides think the girl they're dating will love the backcountry as much as they do. They think their girlfriends will want to get into the business with them. But be realistic. Guiding and outfitting involve a lot of long hours of hard work. They offer few luxuries (such as warm showers or indoor toilets), and provides little economic security. Those things are rarely important to most guides, but over the long haul they mean a lot to most women. Few wives or girlfriends will want that kind of life in the long run.

Again, it's difficult to run an outfitting business without a dedicated spouse helping you. But wives cut out for such a lifestyle are rare. More often than not, guides who get married don't last long in the business, so make that decision carefully.

And if you're not married but have a girlfriend, beware. There will be lots of headaches and heartaches — both for you and the outfitter (and the clients) when you let her take your focus off your work. You may end up having to choose between the two.

Out-Walking The Client

It's a familiar scenario. The young, well conditioned guide climbs along at a comfortable pace — comfortable for him, anyway. He tries to walk slowly, at a pace that's comfortable for the client. But without actually realizing it, he finds that it's harder to walk slowly than to climb at his normal pace. Walking slowly requires a deliberate, conscious effort on his part.

Before long, again without realizing it, the guide lapses back into his normal gait. As he nears the crest of a steep ridge, he's anxious to get to the top. The client is about out of gas. The guide wants to see what's just over the ridge. The client wants to catch his breath.

Forgetting his better judgment, the guide forges on to the top of the ridge, thinking he'll look for game while the client catches up. He knows the client would like a rest, but he figures they've stopped enough times already. "No sense wasting the best hours of hunting time," the guide figures to himself. "The client can rest when he reaches the top."

The guide eases up to the crest of the ridge, but wants to see more of the other side. A herd of elk is feeding just at the edge of a patch of timber, but not where the guide expects them. As he eases forward to get a better view down into a clearing, a sentry cow spots him and barks a warning. The herd breaks into a run, and the guide frantically waves for his hunter to hurry.

Huffing and grunting for all he's worth, the client finally catches up to the guide. If he sees the game at all, it will likely be just a glimpse of tan rumps as they disappear into the timber. If he's lucky, he may get a quick look at a bull before it disappears on the run at long range. And even if he has time to find the bull in his sights, he'll be breathing too hard for a steady aim.

Most anyone who's been a guide for very long has been caught in such a situation. It's easy to slip into inadvertently. Unfortunately, that may be the only chance your client gets at game on what may be his once-in-a-lifetime dream hunt. Or maybe that hunter would have been a repeat client if his guide hadn't out-walked him and spooked the game.

The problem isn't always that of spooking game before clients catch up. More often it's a matter of just plain walking them too hard through the course of a hunt. All too often guides keep up a continuous pace that is just too much for the hunter. Even when you have good intentions and are doing your best to get hunters onto game, it's possible to walk them too long and too hard.

It's difficult to go at a client's pace. Walking slowly is difficult. It takes discipline. It takes patience. It takes a deliberate mental effort. It was a difficult lesson for me to learn as a guide, and I wore out several clients in the process. But it was an important lesson, and I improved as a guide once it was finally driven home.

It's hard to find the right balance between doing your best to get clients onto game and yet staying within their limits. That balance point varies from one client to the next, and you'll have to learn to read each client accordingly. Walking a client too long or hard keeps him from enjoying his guided trip. It's possible to give him his money's worth without walking him into the ground.

Out-shooting the Client (Or Out-fishing Him)

Worse yet is when the guide shoots game that a client may have had a chance at. For that reason, most outfitters won't let their guides carry rifles. At least the wise ones won't. Most states prohibit guides from hunting in competition with clients, and without a firearm a guide has no chance of creating that problem.

Some outfitters feel it's necessary for guides to go armed, and sometimes it is. But even with just a pistol, a guide I know of shot an elk he'd bugled in before the client had a chance at it. The outfitter fired the guide and packed him out of camp the next day, but the damage was already done.

The same goes for fishing guides. In some cases the guide will carry a rod along with him in order to demonstrate technique. Unfortunately, some also take the best holes for themselves and out-fish the clients they're supposed to be teaching to fish. It's best just to keep your line out of the water and concentrate on giving your client what he's paying for.

The list could go on. There are plenty of other problems that guides encounter or create. Booking agents hear numerous complaints about various guides that their clients have booked with. These are just a few of the common ones. They can easily be avoided with just a bit of responsibility and common sense.

CHAPTER EIGHT

WOMEN AND GUIDING

Patience. It was patience that paid off.

The guide kept looking, looking, looking — glassing patiently and persistently — into fringes of timber 600 yards across a canyon. The weather had been hot and dry — up in the 80's through the entire hunt. The unseasonal heat was anything but conducive to elk hunting. And not a single elk had been seen.

Tracks had shown up consistently in the dust, though, proof that elk were still using that area. The guide knew that with enough persistent glassing, sooner or later she would see those elk. That's right, *she*. And perhaps it was her patience as a woman that made the difference.

Maybe some men would have shown that patience too, but chances are very few would have. Most would have been desperately covering ground, exhausting every possibility, trying to get their clients at least a look at elk. And not all women would necessarily have that patience either. But this one showed a particular savvy in that respect, and finally she spotted an elk's rump in the shadowy timber. As a result, in the last 20 minutes of daylight on the last day of the hunt, her client dropped a five-point bull.

Obviously, guiding requires far more than just patience, and women are hardly uniquely qualified. Most any woman with guiding experience will tell you she must possess the same qualities and savvy a man needs for guiding — sometimes including physical strength. But the story above shows there are women who *do* have the desire and ability to be guides. And their gender may sometimes even be an advantage.

Changing Traditions

Traditionally, few girls or women have aspired toward hunting, fishing or strenuous backcountry activities — at least not in a serious way. A few always have, but they were indeed few and usually far between. This was partly because they simply weren't encouraged in that direction as were their brothers, husbands, etc. But for the most part they simply pursued other interests.

To an extent that remains true today, but it seems to be changing. In Montana, for example, statistics show that 13% of the state's hunters are women. And hunter safety or hunter education classes that once consisted almost entirely of boys now often include a substantial percentage of girls. True, some of those girls will lose interest along the way, but certainly not all of them will.

I once interviewed a couple of women who were, or had been, outfitters. Both came from the same background — families with no boys — and therefore each grew up taking the place of her father's son. As one put it, "I was my dad's boy, his girl, and his hired man." Each ended up taking over her father's outfit.

Another woman who eventually became a guide told me she had grown up hunting on a farm in Wisconsin, and was *expected* to hunt as

Females were once uncommon among the ranks of hunters and fishermen. That seems to be changing, and now many are becoming guides. (Photo courtesy DeShaw Outfitters)

she grew up. Her father would send her out with a .22 rifle and a single shell, and her mother would tell her, "I'm expecting (not just hoping for) a squirrel for supper tonight." She says it would infuriate her being sent out this way, but she later realized it was for a purpose.

Women once were almost a novelty as hunters and virtually unheard-of as guides. Cases like those just mentioned were rare, but that won't likely be true in the future. As more and more women are encouraged toward hunting and similar pursuits, perhaps more will become guides. A number already have.

Obstacles — The Myth

There are those in society, particularly voices in the media, who would make it appear as if women have always been held back — especially in endeavors traditionally "dominated" by men. Perhaps at times that has been true. But when they say women face obstacles in getting into outdoor pursuits, personally I don't buy it. The only real obstacle most women face in that regard would be a lack of interest or desire on their part.

Once a rarity even as cooks, more and more women now show up in hunting and fishing camps. Many are showing up as guides. (Photo courtesy DeShaw Outfitters)

Many husbands and fathers now encourage wives and daughters to share in their outdoor pursuits. Fayle DeShaw, of Three Forks, Montana, works as a guide, packer and all-around hand alongside husband Bill in their outfitting business. (Photo courtesy DeShaw Outfitters)

As a married man, I believe I can safely speak for most husbands and fathers in saying they would love to have their wives or daughters as avid hunting partners. One who has a deep love for the outdoors would love to be able share that part of himself as a mutual interest with his spouse. He would love to share that intense interest with a daughter just as with a son.

Granted, there have always been those few who, for various reasons, resent the thought of women in their camps or amidst their circle of hunting/fishing partners. Some see hunting or fishing as their chance to get out with "the boys" — to party and get drunk. And there are those for whom outdoor pursuits are a means to get away from everyone, including their wives and families. There may even be those for whom hunting and fishing are challenges that confirm their "manliness," at least to themselves.

I know of one such hunter who nearly hit the ceiling when the friends he had booked a hunt with told him the outfitter's wife would be in camp as a cook. He thought her presence would have a stifling effect on the partying and ribald camp talk he anticipated. But after she out-rode him, out-walked him, shot several grouse for supper on the way into camp, then continued proving herself throughout the hunt, that hunter wouldn't dream of booking another trip without knowing she would be along. And he came on a lot more hunts.

In my experience, such men are rare, although some do exist. Most often, though, they're stereotypes kept alive by feminists, media, anti-hunters, and the few who actually fit that image. But even those who fit that description will usually change their views when confronted with a woman who demonstrates her competence.

When it comes to guiding, as former guide Paula Del Guidice told me, "Few people believe a woman can and *wants to* do it." That preconception may be a nuisance any woman would have to contend with if she wanted to become a guide. But that hardly stands in her way. It simply requires that she prove herself. Again, the only *true* obstacle a woman would face in becoming a guide is a lack of real interest or desire on her part.

Lack of Opportunity — Another Misconception

Again, there are those who would like women to think they have been, and are being, denied opportunities. In some cases, perhaps that is true, but hardly with most outdoor pursuits. Most people are encouraging women to get involved and are glad to see it when they do. Virtually everyone — sporting clubs, equipment manufacturers, sporting goods dealers, publishers, conservation groups, even outfitters — all stand to benefit when women get involved. They want women to have those opportunities.

Naturally, guiding opportunities will be limited for a woman, because they're limited for everyone. Opportunities are rare enough for any would-be guide. It's not a job to be given to just anyone. As always, the opportunities that exist will be available only to those who take initiative and wrangle them up for themselves. That includes women.

There is always demand for competent guides, be they man or woman. You may have to work hard at rustling up opportunities, and you will have to prove yourself — every guide does. But you *can* find or create those opportunities as long as you're willing to tackle the challenges.

Challenges

Liz Barker, who runs Ford Creek Outfitters near Augusta, Montana, once told me that outfitting is difficult for a man and therefore is difficult for a woman too. The same goes for guiding. Plenty of challenges confront any guide, and women certainly face a few special challenges.

The first, as already stated, is that of proving themselves. Every guide has to prove himself, and women are no exception. The difference is that a woman may have twice the burden of proof, and she may have to prove herself twice as fast. Like it or not, she's bucking tradition and stereotypes. That won't keep her from getting jobs — or opportunities — but it means she'll have to show she can cut the mustard.

The first place any guide must prove up is with the outfitter. Unless he's just plain desperate, an outfitter must either trust you or at least see potential in you before he'll hire you. When he puts you in charge of his equipment, stock or clients, his entire business rides on your competence as a guide.

The next place a woman must prove herself as a guide is when she meets the client. As Del Guidice said, few people believe a woman has the ability or the *desire* to be a guide. She adds that, "In a guiding situation, the onus is on you twice as much." Unless he knows what he's getting into ahead of time, when a male client is paired with a female guide, he may be reluctant to trust her at first. But not necessarily for the reason you might expect.

Men will often be surprised when they encounter a female guide, and at first they may question your ability. However, as licensed guide Fayle De Shaw says, "Once you get them back in the mountains, right away they realize you know more than they do." The biggest problem, though, will be the blow to their pride.

Logically, most men should realize that a woman with experience is every bit as capable of guiding them as a man is. As one female guide said, "I'm not telling them what to do, I'm just showing them where to go." However, if most men got to the root of their initial reluctance, it would probably be simply that they don't want to be shown up.

In traditionally male endeavors, it may be humbling at first for a man to realize a woman knows more than he does. Again though, once the guide proves herself, there should be little problem. She'll have to prove up right off the bat though. I once heard a woman complain at a guides' rap session that men were hesitant to trust her as a guide. The response of an experienced and well known outfitter was simply, "You'll have to

Will he trust you? Right or wrong, a female guide's foremost challenge may be proving herself to the clients.

prove yourself twice as fast."

Even if a guide has proved herself to the client, he still may not actually trust her as long as he can consult one of the male guides. Fayle DeShaw says she has given fly-fishing clients sound advice, but they were reluctant to accept it from her. When they caught up to her husband's drift boat, the client would ask him instead — and get exactly the same advice.

Another challenge women guides may face is the need for physical strength. Like it or not, the fact remains that women aren't designed for upper body strength. And many times a guide's job requires that strength.

In backcountry situations, guides must often pack heavy loads on horses or mules, stack hay, cut, split and carry firewood for camp, and tend to many other chores requiring long hours of heavy physical work. And granted, some women are capable of putting in that kind of labor — especially if they've grown up on ranches and are accustomed to such work and have built up the strength needed for it.

However, most women just don't have the strength needed, say, to lift a 120-pound elk quarter onto a packhorse on the side of a steep, slick, snow-covered mountain. (Heck, plenty of men don't either.) Or how many could get heavy packs loose and get stock untangled and back on its feet when a packstring went down while crossing a stream or in the middle of a dead-fall tangle?

One woman guide told me that the guys on the crew are always ready and eager to jump in and cover if the loads get too heavy for her. And I'm sure that would be the case on most crews. But most outfitters just can't afford to cut an extra man loose to help pack game in or to cover on other heavy work. They usually need a whole crew that is physically capable of handling *every* task.

Another challenge is that of serving the client without making him uncomfortable. Most men have been raised to be somewhat "chivalrous" — at least once-in-a-while. As a result they have difficulty accepting help from a woman. Del Guidice says men were reluctant to accept her offers to carry their rifles, and were even a bit "protective" of her. DeShaw says she has to try not to make men uncomfortable, for example, when dressing game for them — something they would readily let a male guide do.

Women who want to guide will face their share of extra challenges. Hiring a woman may mean an outfitter would have to set up an extra tent for her to live in — which might also mean cutting a lot more firewood. It may mean his clients won't trust him or will be reluctant to eat "humble pie," knowing they'll be paired with a woman more competent than they are. It may mean the necessity of having an extra man covering on heavy lifting. Those factors could become setbacks when hiring is done.

Those women who prove themselves and get the job will have to prove themselves again to the client. Some clients may express distrust in order to cover their stubborn pride. Some may be reluctant to accept a woman's help. And some may act fatherly, or worse, condescending, referring to the guide as "honey" or some similar patronizing term.

Other challenges that guides routinely face could be doubly bothersome for some women. For example, crude sanitation in backcountry camps, lack of shower facilities, and sometimes limited privacy. Demanding, condescending or patronizing clients may come down doubly hard on a woman, increasing the stress of trying to produce when the fish aren't biting or the hunting goes bad. But a woman who wants to guide can overcome those extra challenges. And she may find that in some ways being a woman has its advantages.

The right attitude and mental approach are the key to guiding's challenges for a woman. Del Guidice says that on her first hunt as a guide, she promised herself she wouldn't complain no matter what. She found that when conditions turned sour, the hunting got hard, and the temperatures dropped far below zero, she was the only one in camp who didn't complain.

The Positive Side

Although women are generally not built for strength the way men are, their make-up — both physically and psychologically — can sometimes give them an advantage. Again, rather than trying to prove she can "be a man," a woman in the guiding business should take advantage of her strengths as a female. They can sometimes be a real asset.

For example, one writer has suggested that because men have greater

Once the game is on the ground, can you field dress it without making male clients uneasy? While they might readily let a male guide dress game for them, they'll feel guilty letting a woman do it. (Photo courtesy DeShaw Outfitters)

In backcountry camps, even deluxe sanitation facilities are functional at best. They're often crude, affording little privacy — at best a nuisance for female guides.

strength and stamina, a higher metabolic rate, and a longer and more efficient stride, they move faster and farther than women do when hunting. That's sometimes an advantage, but they also may see less, plus they'll scatter more scent and create more noise. In contrast, a woman moving more slowly will likely pick up more visual detail, scatter less scent and make less noise.

It has also been suggested that while men tend to get a better grasp of the big picture, women by nature tend to pick up more detail and color contrast. Combined with a woman's tendency to move more slowly and patiently, that eye for detail can be an extra advantage in many guiding situations.

Certain personality traits common to women can often be an asset as well. In contrast to the driving personality so common in men, a woman's patience can sometimes be more effective. As mentioned at the start of the chapter, Fayle DeShaw's patient, persistent glassing finally resulted in her spotting a respectable bull elk for her client, while the other guide (her husband) and his client were out covering country. It won't always work that way, but sometimes it pays off.

Those differences can often be an asset when dealing directly with clients as well. DeShaw has found that her laid-back personality is sometimes an advantage compared to her husband's drive. She tends to sense a client's need to rest and relax at times, while her husband constantly pushes them to drift a fly into a likely looking hole as they float a trout stream, or to work out a timbered draw while hunting big game.

Each personality has its good points, and each can be effective when matched up with the appropriate client. The "driver" may often have a better success rate on getting fish or game, but the laid-back type may sometimes be surprisingly effective too. And their clients may often get far more enjoyment from their trip experience, regardless of kill ratios.

The physical differences have paid off as well for DeShaw, who works with her husband. She has found that when clients are older or overweight and less geared toward pushing physically, they often tend to gravitate toward her. Being more inclined to hunt or fish at a pace better suited to such clients, she proves a real asset to their outfitting business.

Advice From Female Guides

If you're expecting unique or specialized advice in this section, forget it. When I asked women with guiding experience what advice they had for other women who want to become guides, they gave the same advice any guide would give a man in that position:

Be ready to work hard and to work long hours. Be in good physical shape. Be knowledgeable about horses and/or mules. Have a positive mental outlook, and be prepared to handle mental stress when things go wrong or the hunting/fishing is lousy. Know the country. Know how to handle bad weather, and how to survive under adverse conditions. Know the habits and habitat of game, and how to hunt that game. The same goes for fish. Develop good game eyes. Know how to handle four-wheel-drive rigs, or stock rigs. Know any basic mechanics you can learn — at least how to change a tire and hook up trailers.

The list could go on from there. Again, it's all good advice for any would-be guide, the same for women as for men.

Many women have sharp eyes for game. They may see more detail and color contrast than men generally do — a definite plus when spotting wildlife.

The Rewards

In the same way, the rewards found in guiding are also the same for women as for men. Fayle DeShaw says above all that she simply enjoys being out on the rivers or in the mountains. She's not there to prove she can lift or work better than the men. She just enjoys being out there.

Del Guidice gave much the same response. For her the people she worked with and hunted with were wonderful, and above all it simply gave her another excuse to get out and hunt. She found satisfaction in helping another hunter get a trophy. She enjoyed doing something she does well, and she enjoyed the challenges of guiding — even having to prove herself.

Behind all the glamour most folks perceive when they think of guides, there's a lot of hard work, trying circumstances and sacrifice. But people still want to live that life, and those who have left it behind always miss it. There are plenty of rewards in a guiding career, for a woman the same as a man.

Getting Started

It's not necessarily easy for a woman to get started in guiding. Most women I've encountered in the business either were raised in it, like the female outfitters mentioned earlier, or got into it of necessity, like Fayle DeShaw. Fayle and her husband started their outfitting business right after they were married, and within three years she had her guide's license and was guiding hunters and fishermen. Her reason? Reliable, competent guides were too hard to find, so she became one herself.

DeShaw was already cooking, packing and dealing with clients anyway, so it was no big step for her to become a guide. She had grown up hunting with her father and had also grown up working with horses. But not all women start out that way.

Del Guidice is a professional writer and hunted with an outfitter as the basis for a publicity write-up she was doing for him. After proving herself on two different hunts she was asked to guide bighorn sheep hunters for him. Former Montana guide Phyllis Friesen got her start in much the same way, as a photo stringer for a large newspaper.

Del Guidice advises women who want to guide to get started much the way she did, by first doing trips with the outfitter as a chance to prove themselves. There are other ways to go about it, as mentioned earlier in the book. No matter what approach a woman takes there will be plenty of challenges to face. First and foremost will be proving herself, but a guide should relish that challenge. As Del Guidice says, "I don't mind being told I have to prove myself." It's all part of the challenge of being a guide.

Alaskan guide Deb Overly of Pioneer Outfitters has shown that a woman who wants to guide can do well in even the toughest country and conditions. (Photo courtesy Jack Atcheson and Sons, Inc.)

CHAPTER NINE

THE FUTURE OF GUIDING

The shrill, hollow notes of a bull elk's bugle pierced the stillness of an early fall morning. With it, like a surge of electricity, came a sudden burst of adrenaline and anticipation. My client and I wanted action. We sensed it was about to start.

I quickly issued a challenge through my grunt tube. To our disappointment, it was never answered. I tried again, with no success. We moved in toward the bull in hopes he would feel his territory encroached upon and would come to challenge us. Still he wouldn't respond to my bugling.

So I changed my tactics, having a new-fangled trick up my sleeve. Pulling a cow call from my pocket, I made sounds of female elk as we worked toward where we had last heard the bull. Sure enough, the rutting bull soon showed himself, and my hunter put him on the ground.

Cow calls were brand new at that time. Sixty years before that, even elk bugles were virtually undreamed-of. I know of an old-time packer who once used a home-made bugle to call a bull across a river into a legal hunting area for one of his clients. The old guide had fashioned his bugle in the early 1900's using a domestic goat horn and a clarinet reed.

When that old outfitter had made his own bugle, hardly anyone even thought about calling elk. Commercial bugles were unheard-of. By the 1950's and 60's, most guides were making their own bugles from plastic pipe. By the 1970's and early '80's, commercially made elk bugles were in widespread use. No early-fall elk guide would have dreamed of leaving camp without a bugle by that time.

By the time I first used a cow call to lure a bull in, so many different bugles were on the market (and still are) that someone just learning to

Hunting and fishing may be the heart of the guiding industry, but don't put all your eggs in one basket. The guide who diversifies will have a brighter future. (Photo courtesy Scott Boulanger)

bugle elk wouldn't know where to begin. But few guides had heard of cow calls and even fewer were using them. A year or two before that time no one had dreamed of using cow sounds when hunting elk. Now, hardly ten years later, few hunters and certainly no elk guide would consider going out without bugles *and* cow calls.

That's one simple example of how guiding is changing. There's no telling what gadgets, technology, and new methods the future may hold. There's no telling just how management policies, the resources themselves, and the clientele will differ. But the fact is that guiding has changed through the years, and it will continue to change in many ways. Most of us hate to see those changes come, but they are inevitable nonetheless.

It is impossible to foresee every change the future holds, but some may be predictable. Those who can anticipate them will be better able to survive and succeed in the guiding industry. But those who fail to "roll with the punches" and adapt to the times will find themselves playing

In several western states, bear seasons have been cut back in recent years. Some changes may be for the better, but they reflect the precarious nature of a livelihood based just on hunting. (Photo courtesy Scott Boulanger)

catch-up at best. Those who just plain refuse to adapt will be left in the dust.

Hunting and Fishing: Putting All Your Eggs in One Basket

If you're like most would-be guides, you want to get into the business for one reason: you like to hunt and fish. Or, in some cases, maybe it's more because you like the thought of working with horses all the time or working in the backcountry. An outfitter who runs one of the more successful guide schools says that virtually every letter he receives from a prospective student starts out, "I have hunted and fished all my life . . . Now I want to become a guide . . ."

Hunting and fishing are still undoubtedly the backbone of the outfitting industry. It's simply easier to sell an outfitted trip to someone intent on pursuing fish or game than to sell scenic pack or float trips as family vacations. However, at the same time, it's difficult to make a living on strictly hunting or fishing business. Most outfitters find they must also offer cabin rentals, trail rides, scenic pack trips, snowmobile trips, or other outfitted services in order to make their business stay afloat. The foreman for an outfitter who did a lot of summer pack trips once told me that it took all the summer business just to pay the bills. Whatever hunting business the outfitter took in was simply his profit margin.

Some outfitters try to make a living just with hunting or just with fishing trips. But invariably, those outfitters also have another form of livelihood. And chances are they still have a hard time making a short season pay for itself. It's all the more difficult for a guide to survive if he only wants to guide those who hunt or fish. So the first strike against hunting and fishing from a guiding standpoint is their seasonal nature. But there are other factors that also make it shaky ground.

One of those factors is the changing demographics of those sports. There are simply more people hunting and fishing and fewer resources for them to use as the years go by. Even the remote backcountry, which was once used only by salty old packers, is now frequently used by locals who have stock of their own and the time and money to use it. Consequently, there is often greater pressure on the game and fish populations, especially on public lands.

This often translates into shorter seasons (which means users of the resources become even more heavily concentrated during that shorter time) or more restrictive bag limits. It can mean point-count restrictions or even hunting only by permits issued in lottery drawings, both of which can make bookings difficult for outfitters.

Changing demographics not only mean increased pressure on the resources, they also show an increasing urbanization of today's culture. Fewer kids have the opportunity to grow up roaming around with a shotgun or a .22 or even a fishing pole on their bicycles. Many people — even teachers in public schools — portray firearms and hunting, and even fishing, as being inherently evil. As a result, a diminishing percentage of the population will likely pursue what are considered "consumptive" forms of recreation in the future.

Understandably, more and more people want to get into the outfitting business. However, as that number increases, the number of hunters and fishermen who hire outfitters is spread increasingly thin. On top of that, more and more other forms of recreation are increasingly available and affordable, spreading the potential hunting or fishing clientele even thinner.

There are few rewards like the satisfaction of guiding a client to hunting success. If you want to be a guide because you love to hunt or fish, do it while the getting is good. But don't bet your future on it. (Photo courtesy Rob Johnson)

Sadly, there's another factor that must be seriously taken into account. As alluded to earlier, many people today perceive guns, as well as any killing of animals, as inherently wrong. Some of these people are passively anti-hunting or fishing simply due to the increasing urbanization of our society. They weren't brought up with it, and therefore they don't like it. Unfortunately, a small but very vocal minority has become actively and rabidly anti- hunting and fishing.

That vocal minority will not likely have a large immediate impact on hunting or fishing. However, as society becomes more urbanized, they may sway more of the passive majority who have grown up totally unexposed to the outdoors. And as more products of our urbanized society fill the ranks of government management and policy-making positions, that vocal minority, which now chips at our foundations, may eventually make powerful inroads against hunting and fishing — especially the commercial side of it, which includes guides.

Most every outfitter I've talked to on the subject believes the future of outfitting (and guiding) lies in areas other than hunting or fishing. Even today, work for hunting and fishing guides is seasonal at best. Those who learn ways to earn a living in the off-season are better off even now, and they'll certainly be better off in the future as "consumptive" recreation opportunities diminish.

If you want to become a guide simply because you like to hunt or fish, I would say go for it. Do it now, while the getting is good. (Just remember that a lot of a guide's job has little or nothing to do with actual hunting or fishing.) But don't stake your future as a guide on it. You'll be putting all your eggs in one basket.

Year-Round Recreation and Tourism

An outfitter who runs a guide school, and therefore is in the placement business, says the average guide's career lasts only three years. Probably the main reason so many outfitters have difficulty finding good guides and keeping them nowadays is that guides just can't make a living at seasonal work. The answer for both outfitters and guides is to branch out into other areas of tourism that will keep them working year-round.

Skiing, sleigh rides, and snowmobile rentals are three obvious possibilities for both outfitters and guides, especially in areas with high winter-tourist traffic. I know a guide who once worked in southwestern Colorado for an outfitter who offered sleigh rides. Business was only heavy enough to keep him working part-time, but that left him plenty of time to ski. By gaining the necessary knowledge, training and experience, a guide in such an area might pick up work as a ski instructor or on a ski patrol.

Cross-country skiing is another area with real potential for outfitters and guides. Due to its relatively low cost, it is something many families can get involved in, and some individuals become outright enthusiasts. Rental cabins with groomed ski trails, or even guided ski tours to backcountry cabins, are a possibility for guides with the right experience and know-how.

Another option for guides who lack the experience or desire to get into snow-related recreation might be to work up north through the summer and fall, then work in the extreme Southwest through the winter months. Many dude ranch/resorts in the desert Southwest offer most of their pack trips and trail rides during the winter months, when temperatures are moderate, rather than in the hot summer months.

Those are only a few of the many year-round possibilities that outfitters, and especially guides, may want or need to branch into as the industry and its clientele change through the future. The possibilities are unlimited. The only question is which services clients will pay for. There's little question, however, that guides will have to diversify as hunting and fishing opportunities diminish.

Non-Consumptive Recreation

In reality the term "non-consumptive" is misleading. No recreation is really non-consumptive. Although the term is often used somewhat self-righteously by those who don't take game or fish out of the existing populations, in reality those people are still consuming something from the resource.

At best, by their very presence, those recreationists are consuming some of the solitude and wildness that would be more readily enjoyed by others if those "non-consumptive users" stayed home. Just the same, those forms of recreation deemed non-consumptive are gaining in popularity, and the future of guiding may lead that direction.

Again, most outfitters I've talked to believe various forms of non-consumptive recreation will eventually be crucial to the industry's future. Although potential "consumptive use" clientele is being spread increasingly thin, the general population appears to be developing an increasing interest in outdoor recreation. "Outdoors" and "wilderness" are fashionable. An outfitter or guide who can tap into that interest may well be the one who succeeds in the future.

Naturally, the winter pursuits discussed under "year-round recreation," are one type of non-consumptive use. However, guides and outfitters should hardly limit their non-consumptive recreation services to the off-season. Again, as consumptive opportunities and clientele diminish, non-consumptive pursuits may have to take up the slack, even during the regular hunting or fishing season.

As people develop more of an interest in nature, conservation and ecology, interpretive pack or float trips may become more popular — trips in which the clients are actually taught the history and natural history of an area rather than simply shown how or where to catch lots of fish or kill game. Such trips would require guides to know the history and biology of the area themselves, but such knowledge would also make them better "consumptive" guides.

Wildlife and nature photography are increasingly popular as well. Even some "consumptive" users, eventually prefer to hunt with a camera rather than a firearm. Or perhaps hunters simply want to take a trip with non-hunting friends. Photo "safaris" are one promising area. One outfitter I worked for does very well with photo-oriented pack trips into elk country during bugling season. Such trips sometimes even take priority over his hunting trips.

Again, non-consumptive possibilities for guides are limited only by outfitters' imaginations, what clients are willing to pay for, and the extent to which guides are willing to learn and diversify. But as consumptive opportunities dwindle and non-consumptive opportunities increase, the guide who makes a living long-term will be the one who diversifies.

Low-Impact Camping and Land Use

Regardless of what other changes take place in the industry, any guide who deals with clients on public land will have to know low-impact camping and/or horse use techniques. It's guaranteed. For years, public land administrators such as the U.S. Forest Service have been encouraging users to minimize their impact on the resources. As time goes along, more and more of those suggestions will become law.

Just last year (1994), for example, the U.S. Forest Service nearly began requiring all horse packers to keep all food in bear-proof containers. And in many districts, due to threat of noxious weeds choking out wildlife range, the Forest Service has also started requiring that any hay brought in by packers be certified "weed-free."

Most reputable outfitters and guides have long realized their need to minimize their impact on the resource. Their future livelihood depends on it, not to mention the value of that resource to other users. However, as more and more private use is concentrated on public lands, increased impact is inevitable.

With increased impact, more regulations will be placed on both outfitted and private use. Minimum-impact practices will eventually be required, whether we like it or not. It's crucial that guides learn and adopt low-impact practices on their own, in order to keep our wild resources wild. If they don't, those requirements will be forced on them all the sooner.

Versatility/Flexibility: Maintaining Traditional Use While Looking Toward the Future
When a client books a horseback trip, he's looking for an image.

This guide demonstrates various low-impact camping techniques to U.S. Forest Service employees. With increasing demands on a limited resource, all guides must learn to minimize their impact.

Changing times. Llamas have filled a niche among backcountry travellers, proving ideal for low-impact packing. Most guides will encounter them on mountain trails, or even use them eventually. (Photo courtesy Great Northern Llama Co.)

Even on just a summer pack trip he's looking for cowboys, a taste of the Old West, whether he realizes it or not. True, when many fishing clients hire guides, all they're looking for is a chance to catch as many fish as possible with the most efficient, modern gear. But still, even those clients like local flavor.

When most clients hire a guide, they want a touch of nostalgia, a taste of the region's history. They want a taste of the way things used to be. They want to "rough it," to an extent; they just don't want it too rough. The more modern conveniences those clients can have, the better. Just so they think they're getting a taste of things the way they once were.

To most clients that means nothing. And to most land-use administrators it means very little. But for outfitters and guides it means a real dilemma.

As public land use increases, the accompanying regulations increase with it. As the demographics of our society change, demand for various types of outfitted or guided services will change too. And as new gadgets, technology, and synthetic materials are developed, different types of gear and techniques will come into use. That's where a guide's dilemma lies. He must try to maintain the tradition his industry is based on, but he must also be versatile enough to adapt it to changing demands, clientele, regulations, and technology.

Lighter-weight camp gear and techniques that reduce impact may become an increasing necessity. But clients will still want a nostalgic slant too. Knowledge of photography, natural history, skiing, or various other forms of non-consumptive recreation may also become necessities for a guide. Guides must adapt, but they still must maintain a touch of the regional tradition that their clients couldn't find where they came from.

Hunting and fishing will undoubtedly remain the backbone of the guiding industry for a long time to come. But the industry's future may eventually lead toward diversification. Tradition will always remain at the heart of the industry, but again, those who stick only to hunting or fishing will have all their eggs in one basket. Guides willing to be flexible and versatile — to adapt and diversify — may well have a brighter future.

You won't get rich as a guide, but you'll find it offers rewards that don't show up in the bank account. (Photo courtesy Rob Johnson)

CHAPTER TEN

WHAT'S IN IT FOR ME?

By now you may be convinced that guiding involves nothing but self-sacrifice — sacrificing physical effort, sleep, personal preferences and luxuries as well as the chance to work at a better-paying job — all this simply to make life enjoyable for the client. And that client will oftentimes be inept, and occasionally even demanding and ungrateful.

However, there must be something more to it. If those who are guides seem to love it the way they do, and so many others wish they could become guides, it must be rewarding in some way.

Although guiding is a "servant's" profession — a giving rather than a receiving profession — it certainly has its perks. Getting down to the "bottom line," guiding really is a rewarding occupation, and it is possible to earn something of a livelihood at it. Here are some thoughts on what's in it for you.

Will I Get to Hunt or Fish Myself?

Not long ago I read a magazine article featuring several outfitters. It mainly discussed the problems and realities of their profession — aspects that people on the clients' side of the fence never think about. Probably the most common complaint among the outfitters was that finding good, dependable guides was always a problem. They complained that all the guides wanted to do is go out and hunt themselves.

One of the ironies of guiding is that most guides get into the profession because they love to hunt or fish, yet they get very little time to do those things themselves. They're always busy with all the various tasks that go into setting up quality camps, getting clients into those

If he's lucky, a guide may get a few days to hunt on his own. But don't count on it. Outfitters must pack as many clients as possible into a limited season. If the guides get to hunt or fish, it's a bonus.

camps, then guiding those clients and tending to the limitless after-hours chores that make a client's trip first-class.

When it comes to hunting or fishing, an outfitter can do business only during the limited time that the seasons are open. Quite often, in backcountry situations, there's an even shorter time period in which he can actually count on his territory being accessible. Mountain passes are usually snowed in well into summer, and they snow in again fairly early in the fall. High water makes river crossings dangerous and limits backcountry travel during spring and early-summer run-off.

Time becomes money in those cases. The outfitter will cram as many hunting or fishing clients as possible into that limited season, which means his guides will generally be tied up during that entire time. If they manage to get any time to hunt or fish, it will often be only during rare and stolen opportunities on the days between trips.

However, one redeeming factor is that most outfitters continually have to struggle in order to fill their bookings. They'll often end up with a certain amount of slack time at some point in the season, and some will

Putting clients onto game offers twice the challenge of hunting on your own. You may not squeeze the trigger yourself, but you get to hunt the entire season — and get paid to do it! (Photo courtesy Scott Boulanger)

let their guides take advantage of that time to do some hunting themselves.

Most outfitters will feel an obligation to the clients, and they won't let their guides hunt in their territories until all the clients have left. But occasionally guides will get a few days of hunting time. Don't necessarily count on it though. It varies from one outfit to another.

Sometimes fishing can be a different story, depending on the outfitter and the clients he deals with. If you're hired specifically as a fishing guide for day trips and float/fishing trips, your time will probably be taken up with guiding and handling the boat or raft. Any chance you get to fish yourself will just be a bonus.

However, on backcountry pack-in trips, clients often fall into either of two categories. Often they're such novices that the fishing is secondary, and they're mainly along for the horseback/mountain experience. Or else they're serious fishermen who already know what they're doing and are along mainly just to get into good fishing. These usually want your services more as a packer than as a guide.

Consequently, on lay-over days, when you're not busy packing and setting up camps, you might well find some time to fish. Again though, don't count on it much.

I've often heard it said of guiding hunters that when you're guiding, you hunt; you just don't get to pull the trigger. The same could be said for guiding fishing clients. You not only get to do what you enjoy, it's all the more challenging.

It's at least twice as difficult to get a hunter — usually one far less skilled that you are — into position to get a shot at a good buck or bull. Perhaps it's even more so when guiding fly fishermen, especially novices. There are plenty of challenges in getting a beginner to cast well and present a fly just right and set the hook at just the right time. You still get to execute the stalk or read the stream. You just don't get to squeeze the trigger or set the hook and land the fish.

If meat is a big concern, oftentimes you'll find that hunters will offer you part of their meat rather than pay the high cost of shipping it home. A couple of seasons ago I didn't get to hunt a single day, but hunters I had guided gave me more than enough meat to make up for what I might have gotten otherwise.

Realistically, we all know that guiding just isn't quite the same as hunting for yourself. It's tough to explain, but there's something lacking when you don't get the opportunity to squeeze the trigger or land the fish. It's not quite the same when you don't get the chance to succeed or fail, to culminate the effort yourself.

That's one of the trade-offs of being a guide, though. You may have to sacrifice the chance to hunt or fish like you want to, but in return you get to spend every day in good country, directly involved with what you enjoy. You may often have to sacrifice a pastime, but in exchange you get a way of life.

One outfitter I worked for had achieved the best of both worlds in this regard. Having done a lot of hunting and been quite successful on his own before getting into the business, he no longer desired to kill game. He just enjoyed being out and taking the clients out. He was content just to experience the hunt and enjoy hunting vicariously through the success of the clients he guided.

If you have reached that point, you're fortunate, but most hunters never do. Usually the only way to reach that point is to do enough hunting or fishing that it becomes commonplace to you. It's much like the dilemma of needing experience in order to get a job but not being able to get it until you're hired. It's tough to get that much hunting or fishing done when you're busy guiding. Instead you have to learn to enjoy bringing other people to success. Any additional chance you get to hunt or fish on your own is just a bonus.

Finances

At the end of a season, it's not uncommon for a guide to have more money than the outfitter does. But that hardly means he's better off. At least the outfitter owns his business, or has a certain amount of equity built up in it. All a guide usually has is whatever wages he's saved during the season. Still, that can sometimes amount to quite a bit.

The outfitter can look forward to a certain amount of cash flow. But unless the guide has some sort of off-season employment he can fall back on, or at least some family or friends he can bunk up with, he may be looking at a long, lean winter. He'd better have saved up his wages.

As I've already tried to emphasize, guides' pay is often low. Whether you figure it in terms of the hours worked or in terms of how

The lifestyle, experiences, and camaraderie guides enjoy are rewards that can't be measured financially.

far it will stretch, either way it comes out low. And the job is most often seasonal, which limits that income all the more. It can be tough to make a living as a guide.

However, for someone who's industrious, and who's careful with his wages, guiding can be more financially feasible than it may at first sound. First off, as long as a guide is working in the backcountry, he has little chance to spend his wages, which is conducive to saving money. Secondly, the wage structure usually includes room and board. That can save a guide an awful lot of out-of-pocket expense. Thirdly, there's always the possibility of receiving tips. If used wisely rather than squandered, they can often add up to a substantial supplement to your salary. (More on that shortly.)

Guides are usually paid a monthly wage *plus* room and board. By not having to pay rent or buy groceries you're automatically saving a big chunk out of your wages. Occasionally, an outfitter will let a few of his guides stay in his bunkhouse through the winter, even if he can't keep them on the payroll. Once in a great while an outfitter may even let a guide work through the winter for room and board, even if he doesn't have a lot for him to do (especially if he wants to be sure that guide is back next year). And there are a few rare cases where a guide can actually find an outfitter who will keep him employed year-round.

A guide who is willing to be careful with his money may well be able to set aside enough during the season to help him get through the off-season. I once worked with a packer/guide who took in enough tips during the course of a season that he was able to live on them through most of the summer and fall. All his wages went into the bank.

Chances are, though, that most guides would get pretty hungry and their bank accounts would get pretty thin, by the time the next season starts up. Given the need to continually replace or upgrade worn out equipment, it's difficult for a guide to squirrel away as much of his wages as he'd prefer.

In most states, the hunting/packing season is over before the ski runs get going full bore. A guide may stand a chance of finding an off-season job at a ski run that fits ideally into the time he's laid off for the winter and spring. There's also the possibility of finding off-season employment at dude ranches in the Desert Southwest, where the prime tourist season runs during winter and early spring.

I've known of several guides who worked regular jobs as truck drivers, electricians, or carpenters in the eastern or midwestern states from which they came. They were fortunate enough to be able to leave their regular jobs during the hunting season each year in order to come west and work as guides. They would then return to their regular jobs when they were done guiding. Those situations are rare, but the point is that for someone who really wants to work as a guide there are ways to make it financially feasible.

Tips

Unless the service is absolutely terrible, virtually no one would ever think of eating a meal in a restaurant without leaving a tip for the waiter or waitress. And when it comes to guided hunts, fishing trips or pack trips, most guides and most clients have long since heard that it's customary for the client to leave gratuities for the crew, or at least for his guide. However, don't count on it. Some do and some don't.

The best attitude to take when it comes to tips is not to expect them. Like getting to hunt yourself, tips are just an added bonus if you get them. Rather than be disappointed by expecting a tip and not getting it, be pleasantly surprised by getting a tip when you didn't count on it.

Some clients just don't realize that tipping is customary. And in some cases the client just can't afford it after scraping and saving just to take a once-in-a-lifetime dream hunt. With expenses for licenses, travel, lodging, special clothing or gear needed for the trip, not to mention the price of the trip itself, the added burden of a tip may be more than they can bear. Then in some cases the client may just be so cheap, hard-to-please, or downright cantankerous that he'll deliberately neglect to tip you no matter how hard an effort you gave him or how successful his trip may have been.

Tips are often viewed as a customary and necessary supplement to a guide's rather limited income. Most outfitters realize this, especially in light of how little they're able to pay their guides or the limited time that they're able to keep them employed during the year. As a result they sometimes mention tipping in the printed material they send out to prospective clients. Some even pointedly suggest it when discussing the cost of the trip. Again, though, don't count on it. Not all outfitters do this, and even when they do it's just a suggestion, not an obligation.

It's best to keep in mind that a tip is a gratuity, an expression of gratitude. Don't expect a tip if you aren't continually going the extra mile to give your client the best possible experience. You should give 110 percent regardless of your chances of being tipped, but remember, the better effort you put out for your client the better your chances of earning a tip. Put yourself in your client's boots and ask yourself if you would leave a gratuity for the kind of service he's getting.

The size of your tips, or whether you even receive them, often varies from one outfit to another and from one client to another. It often depends on the type of services rendered and the type of client catered to. Naturally, your tips will generally be bigger and more regular when working for a high-priced trophy outfit than if you guide for a take-what-comes, good ole' boy type of outfit.

A magazine's field editor once wrote that the standard for tipping is ten percent of the trip's price, but I doubt I've ever seen that hold true. I've heard of a hunting guide receiving a $1,000 tip, and I also heard of a case where a hunter told his guide he would tip him $100 per point if the guide put him onto an elk. He ended up getting a 6X6. However, more often than not I've seen tips closer to five percent of the trip's price, or even less.

Tips can be a valuable and much appreciated supplement to your

The friendships you'll develop, both with clients and crew members, are perhaps the most rewarding aspect of a guide's job.

income as a guide, But again, don't plan on getting them. Or better yet, plan on not getting them. That way, you'll be pleasantly surprised by any tips you get rather than disappointed over the ones you don't.

Guiding as a Means of Working Your Way Through College

Enough can be said on this subject that I've dedicated the entire next chapter to it. However, while I'm on the subject of what's really in guiding for you, I at least want to mention this possibility.

For someone who doesn't see guiding as a lifetime career but wants to try it before moving to something long-term, guiding has the potential to be a good way of working through college. Again, you will have to be careful with your money, and you'll have to make other sacrifices to make it work. But it worked for me, and it worked for other guides I know. Give it some thought.

The Real Rewards

As I stated early in this book, the real rewards in guiding are not monetary. In other words, it pays lousy. Although I was being facetious, I was also trying to make a couple of serious points. First, in terms of the amount of work a guide must do and the conditions he often works under, the pay really is fairly low. But secondly, guiding can be rewarding in ways far beyond what any amount of money could ever represent.

Guiding offers not only the satisfaction of hard work and, to an extent, self-sufficiency and self-reliance, but also the satisfaction of giving or sharing what people rarely, if ever, experience during their everyday lives. It offers a chance to develop an expertise in areas that most folks yearn just to get a taste of. It lets you pass that knowledge and expertise on in order to help those folks enjoy it. And it lets you develop and enjoy a camaraderie with clients and crew, all in a setting and environment most folks only dream of.

When people are willing to pay as much as you earn in a month — or often two to three times your monthly wage, and even more — just to experience for a week or ten days what you get paid to do for several months out of the year, then there obviously are rewards in guiding far beyond just the monetary wage.

*It won't be easy, but you **can** wear more than one hat. By using a guiding career to work your way through school, you can enjoy the best of both worlds.*

CHAPTER ELEVEN

GUIDING YOUR WAY THROUGH COLLEGE

On the way back to my dorm room to study after classes, I dropped in to pick up my mail. I could hardly believe what I found. Waiting in the mailbox was my first publication contract for an article I had submitted to a major outdoor magazine. I was elated.

The article I had sold was titled "Getting the Most From Your Guide," and I was successful in selling it for two reasons. I was learning the mechanics of writing while in college, but I could also write it first-hand from a hunting guide's point of view. For several years I had enjoyed the best of both worlds, attending college during winter semesters and earning money to pay the bills by working through the summer and fall as a packer and hunting guide.

What? Guide your way through college? Guides don't go to college, do they? They're just a bunch of uneducated, out-of-work cowboys or loggers who would rather hunt or fish than sit behind a desk, right? Why would a guide stick his nose in the books?

Realistically, it's pretty difficult to make a long-term career of guiding, so college isn't a bad idea for guides. And vice versa. It's tough to make a long-term career in many fields without a degree of some kind, so guiding isn't a bad idea for those who want to go to college. It can be a great way to pay your school bills.

Actually, quite a few guides either have a college education or end up getting one. And you'd be surprised how many outfitters have them. Just about the only way to make a life-long career of guiding is to get into the business as an outfitter, and anyone who hopes to succeed in the outfitting business nowadays has to be pretty sharp. With the demands of the business and its increasingly competitive nature, a college education can be helpful.

When the season ends and snow forces you out of the mountains, that's the time to head off to college. (Photo courtesy Rob Johnson)

A college degree is no guarantee in nowadays' world, and guiding is hardly a sure-fire means of paying your way through school. (What is?) But it worked out well for me as well as several other guides I know, or know of. It just might be the ticket for you.

Turning Negatives Into Positives

For several reasons, guiding is often difficult to stick with as a long-term career. Relatively low wages, the job's seasonal nature, and the extensive time spent in the backcountry are the main reasons. For someone young and single those factors aren't always a problem. But when you take on long-term personal and financial commitments (such as marriage, families, and house payments), which most of us eventually do, those aspects of guiding begin to conflict with your responsibilities.

However, it is possible to turn these negatives into pluses, to turn potential drawbacks to your advantage. The factors that make guiding a tough way to earn a long-term living can actually make it conducive to working your way through college.

Demand

For starters, the relatively low wages and particularly the short seasons make for a high turnover rate amongst guides. After running a guide school and placing new guides on jobs for many years, outfitter Jack Wemple has found that most guides stay in the business for an average of only three years. The positive side is that there is always demand for guides — especially guides who can come back year after year. And guides working through college a semester or a couple of quarters at a time will likely be back over the long haul.

Off-Seasons

A second positive is that, while the seasonal nature of guiding makes it a difficult way to earn a year-round living, it leaves you free to attend college during the off-season. The key is locking in as a packer and guide for an outfitter who does pack trips and fishing trips in the summer and then hunting trips in the fall. This lets you spend half the year earning money for college and still leaves you free for school during winter semester (or winter/spring quarters).

Wage Structure

Still another plus is that the traditional wage structure for guides is conducive to saving for college. Granted, compared to what a guide might be able to earn in a lot of other jobs the wages are sometimes low. But guides' wages most often include room and board, which saves them a big chunk of out-of-pocket expense.

There will be other expenses for clothing, boots, and gear that will eat into a guide's wages, but one who manages his money wisely should be able to save a fair chunk of it for the upcoming school term. If nothing else, he should be able to save what he would otherwise be paying for rent and grub.

Backcountry Bonus

A fourth positive that can be found from guiding's negatives is that spending extended lengths of time in the backcountry keeps a guide from spending his money. This makes saving for school that much easier. There are no convenience stores, fast-food joints, bars, etc. for a guide to waste money in while he's in the backcountry.

As long as he stays out of high-dollar backcountry poker games and doesn't go on spending sprees when he finally hits town, a guide should

A few outfitters keep guides busy through the winter with lion hunts, snowmobiling, etc. Such opportunities are rare, however. Take advantage of off-seasons by going to school. (Photo courtesy Wildlife Adventures, Inc.)

be able to save a big chunk of his wages for school.

True, earning a living long-term as a guide is difficult. The reasons are obvious. But one man's disadvantage can be a real plus for another man. For someone working his way through college, a guide's job can potentially be ideal.

Getting the Job

As mentioned in the first chapter, there are different ways of landing a guiding job, and each has its good and bad points. For someone lacking the necessary experience, there are basically two options. One is simply to contact outfitters until you find one who will hire you and teach you. The other is to go through a school designed to give would-be guides basic knowledge and experience.

The biggest advantage of a well-rounded school is that it can teach you in several weeks of concentrated instruction what might take you several years to learn here-and-there on the job. A good school will teach a variety of techniques, rather than just one man's way of doing things.

And by learning the basics in a school so that the outfitter won't have to take time to teach you, you'll stand a good chance of starting out at a fairly high wage.

Another advantage is that a good school will place its graduates on jobs. It will likely have a waiting list of outfitters looking to hire trained guides.

The disadvantage of schools is that they require a big cash outlay. They're not cheap, and not everyone can easily come by that amount of money. Granted, schools can be a good investment. By landing the right job you can earn back as much in your first season (at least in gross wages) as you paid in tuition. But you still have to lay out a big chunk of cash to start with. And there's no guarantee you'll graduate.

The biggest advantage of hiring on directly with an outfitter is that you avoid laying out the price of tuition that you would pay if going through a school. The main disadvantage is that you would likely start out at a pretty low wage — possibly nothing more than room and board. Many outfitters prefer to start their guides out that way, though. They want to train them their own way from the start.

A lot of outfitters are still leery of guide schools and the quality of student they might turn out. Understandably so. No school can make an experienced guide of anyone, and some schools give very poor training. (Check them out thoroughly!) The fact that someone went through a school doesn't necessarily guarantee he'll be able to cut it in the real guiding world. Also, the fact that a hand has been trained in a guide school doesn't mean he has been taught the way a particular outfitter desires.

However, some outfitters don't feel they have time to spend on training new guides when they could hire one who has already been taught the basics in a good school. These outfitters will likely expect more of the new guide and will give him more responsibility from the start. But they will also be likely to start him at a higher wage.

Again, there are various ways to go about getting a guiding job. Each has its good and bad points. There's no right or wrong way, and what works best for one person might not be best for another. Everyone has to weigh the trade-offs and choose for himself which way is best for him. Good luck!

Getting the Right Job

Don't get the impression that guiding is a sure-fire means of paying college tuition while working at a dream job. Most guiding jobs would not be given to just anyone, and not every guiding job will get you through school. The key is not just getting a job. It's getting the *right* job.

Many outfitters employ guides only during the hunting season. Even those who run summer trips generally need less help at that time than when hunting season gets into full swing. With one of the outfits I've worked for, just the outfitter and two wranglers could easily take care of a dozen guests plus all the stock and equipment needed for an eight-day pack trip. The same number of guests on a guided hunt would require at least twice as much crew.

Also, not all outfitters pay the same wage. And not all guides are experienced enough or responsible, hard-working and savvy enough to merit the same wage. Consequently, jobs that would keep guides working long enough, or pay a high-enough wage, to cover an upcoming semester

In order to earn and save enough money for an upcoming semester of college, you'll have to work at least half the year. Before committing to a job, be sure the outfit does enough summer pack trips, trail rides or float trips to keep you working all summer and fall.

of college are not always just there for the taking.

It may take a season or two of gaining experience and proving yourself in order to work into a job that would get you through school. Your best bet may be to hire on at the start of hunting season, when a larger crew is needed. After learning the outfit's operation and then proving yourself during the fall, you'll be in better position to get hired early when work starts up the next spring or summer.

Just make sure there's a chance of working into a position that will keep you employed for both summer and fall before you hire on. There's no point spinning your wheels with an outfit that hires only for hunting season or just for the summer — not if you want your guiding job to help pay your way through college.

Financial Supplements for Students

Even under the most ideal circumstances most guide/students will find that after expenses take a bite out of wages, they won't have quite enough left to get them through a semester of college. If you're fortunate (or blessed) there will be a certain amount of help from home somewhere along the way. If that's not available, there are other types of financial supplements that can help students short on funds.

Federal and state financial aid, such as Pell Grants and low-interest Guaranteed Student Loans (GSL's) are the better known and most readily available types of funding for students short of tuition money. Virtually all public colleges or universities, and many private ones, have a department dedicated specifically to helping students obtain these types of financial assistance. That office or department at whichever school you choose to attend would be the best source of information on just what is available to you and how to obtain it.

Another good source of financial help is in the form of scholarships. Numerous local and state organizations offer small scholarships to graduating high school students, and most libraries contain books listing national scholarships prospective college students can apply for. Once a student has entered into a specific major, many memorial funds or professional organizations offer scholarships to students pursuing a career in that particular field.

For example, the Outdoor Writers' Association of America offers several substantial scholarships to students majoring in fields such as journalism, wildlife biology, etc. As a professional organization the OWAA desires to help promising students who aspire to careers

If what's left of your season's wages won't cover school expenses, most all schools have a department dedicated toward helping students get scholarships, grants and financial aid.

involving outdoors-related communications. The Rocky Mountain Elk Foundation also offers substantial scholarships to students showing promise in fields related to wildlife conservation. Similar scholarships are available in virtually any field of study.

Unfortunately, most scholarships and financial assistance are skewed against people who are industrious and frugal. The reasoning behind this is based on good intention. The awards are given to those who demonstrate actual need. Sadly, it is often the achievers, who actually deserve such awards, who have worked hard and saved hard and therefore don't qualify based on ability to demonstrate need.

This can work against a guide who is working through school. At the time scholarships are applied for, a guide may be just coming off a season of working in the mountains. If he has saved his wages carefully and done without a lot of the luxuries or fancy gear that's tempting but could be done without, he probably has a sizeable chunk of money in the bank. Chances are it won't get him through a semester of school, but it may keep him from qualifying for grants or scholarships.

For those who are at all industrious, there is another form of scholarship that should be available to anyone. Packer, guide, and artist

Joe Back referred to it in his book *The Old Guide Remembers, The Young Guide Finds Out*. When he went to art school in Chicago, Back found himself short on funds. He managed to wrangle up three different part-time jobs to help him get through school, and that's what he considered his scholarships.

For someone who is willing to work, there are usually jobs to be had around any college. They aren't always the most glamorous, but they pay. The job you find may be custodial work, slinging hash in the dormitory chow-hall, or flipping burgers at a fast-food joint downtown. You may have to earn cash as a lab assistant or in some other academically-related work. But there are usually jobs for students who want to work.

Pitfalls to Avoid

A few points are worth pondering before you plunge headlong into what sounds too good to be true. Although I've mentioned several of these warnings already, I'll repeat them here and add a few more, rather than lead someone down a primrose path. The possibility of guiding your way through college is not too good to be true, but it is also not something to enter into blindly.

First off, there are no guarantees when it comes to getting the right job. Enrolling in a guide school doesn't guarantee you'll pass. Even if you pass, there's no guarantee you'll have the savvy needed in the real world. Some things just can't be taught in schools. And whether you graduate from a guide school or wrangle a job on your own, there's no guarantee it will pay enough to get you through school.

Guides' wages usually run somewhat consistent from one outfitter to another. Still, not all guides will earn (or merit) the same wage, even with the same amount of experience, or within the same outfit. And expenses for necessary clothing and gear will eat into whatever wages you do earn.

Also, not all outfitters keep their guides employed for a long-enough season to get them through school. Just landing a job with any outfitter won't guarantee you'll earn enough wages in a year to cover a semester of school. Every guide starts out under different circumstances, and each one will have different needs when it comes to paying for school.

Not all majors are conducive to attending school a semester at a time, either. Some may require courses to be taken in an immediate sequence. Some schools, particularly smaller schools, may offer certain classes only during certain semesters. If a course required for your major is offered only during fall semester, you may be out of luck, either in terms of guiding that fall or in terms of getting the class you need.

The Best of Both Worlds

Guiding can be a difficult means of working through school. But what way isn't hard? At times guiding your way through college may sound like a dream, too good to be true. But it can be done. And it lets you enjoy the best of both worlds — working seasonally at what may be a "dream" job, and going to school in the off-season, having earned enough (or nearly enough) to pay for that term.

Unlike most things that sound too good to be true, this one actually is possible. It will take a lot of hard work on your part, and it will take plenty of frugality along the way. It will even require the hand of Providence guiding you to the right job. But you *can* enjoy the best of both worlds by guiding your way through college.

Staring into a dwindling fire on some high, lonesome ridge with civilization the farthest thing from your mind. No high-paying job could ever replace such satisfying, hard-earned solitude.

CHAPTER TWELVE

CHOOSING A GUIDE SCHOOL

Not long ago, a retired outfitter showed me an exuberant letter and photograph that he had received from a young guide. The letter described how the new guide had bugled in a five-point bull elk for a client to shoot with a muzzleloader. The young guide later had a chance to use a bugle and muzzleloader to bring down an elk himself. He was overflowing with gratitude.

The letter thanked the outfitter for recommending a school and getting the young man started in guide training. The kid was thrilled with the new experiences of starting out in a fulfilling career (one that most people only dream of). And the outfitter found a lot of satisfaction in helping the young man get started on the right foot.

On the other hand, just a few years ago a would-be guide filed a lawsuit against an outfitter who ran a guide school in my area. The former student claimed in his suit that the school failed to teach what the outfitter said it would. He also claimed that instructors taught the students how to poach, and even showed them how to use a rifle during archery season, then stick an arrow into the wound in order to make it look legal.

The point is that, as with anything in life, there are good outfitters and bad outfitters, and there are good schools for guides as well as bad ones. Attending a quality school can be a good way to get started in a guiding career, but enrolling in a bad school can make for shattered dreams, a waste of hard-earned cash, and a very bitter and unpleasant experience.

There is no way I could recommend any particular guide school over another, or even recommend that would-be guides should even go through a school. However, having gone through a school myself before beginning my guiding career, I will say that it can certainly be a good way to get started. I can also give a few pointers on what to look for, and what to watch out for, when choosing a guide school.

Background Check

A few "caveats," or warnings, apply when choosing a guide school. The first is *"caveat emptor"*: Let the buyer beware.

This isn't to put all guide schools in a bad light. However, at this point most states have no governing board that regulates guide schools. Consequently, virtually anyone can start a guide school regardless of his knowledge, experience or other professional qualifications. At that school he can teach whatever he wants, teach as much or as little as he wants, charge whatever he wants, etc.

Under most states' regulations, in order to run a guide school one would have to have an outfitter's license if the students used any of his livestock, vehicles or gear during their instruction, or if any of the instruction was done on public lands. But for the most part, the only people to whom a guide school operator is really accountable as far as his school itself is concerned would be his students, and possibly their lawyers. That's why a reasonable amount of caution is advised.

Usually, you'll get a pretty good idea just how professional an outfitter is, and how well he'll run a school, just by reading the informational brochures his school sends out. However, once you've narrowed the choices down to the top few schools that interest you, it might not hurt to check into them further.

One way to do this would be a letter or phone call to the local Chamber of Commerce, the state outfitter board, the state Fish and Game department, professional outfitter organizations, or possibly even the U.S. Forest Service or other public land administrators the outfitter deals with. Make sure he is reputable and in good standing with those organizations. Any recommendation or approval by the state's Board of Education wouldn't hurt either, although, as stated before, they may have no knowledge of or control over a given school.

Price

The first outfitter I worked for booked many of his clients by setting up a display booth at a large sports show. From time to time a disgruntled show-goer would stop by his booth and complain about a bad experience he'd had with an outfitter in the past. The outfitter began talking more in depth with these jilted sportsmen in an effort to find out the root of their problems. He found that, almost invariably, the ones who had had bad experiences were those who had tried to book the cheapest possible trips.

The same goes for choosing a guide school. Just as an outfitted hunt or pack trip is not cheap, neither is guide training. An outfitter who cuts too many corners on costs will end up cutting corners on your training — both by nature and by necessity. That doesn't necessarily mean you should choose the most expensive school you can find. But the principle holds true that you get only as much as you pay for.

Length

Most schools I've looked into seem to run an average of about four weeks. Some run a bit longer, a few may run shorter. This is something to take into account when considering prices. To an extent, the length of your resident instruction will be reflected in the school's price. Again, you'll likely get what you pay for.

Another factor to consider is how extensive the instruction will be within the overall session. A school where instruction runs only from eight to five, five days a week may do little to prepare you for the daylight-to-dark, seven-days-a-week schedule that's so often typical of guiding in the real world. At the same time, you may actually learn more in a four-week school that keeps students busy from daylight to dark than in a five- or six-week school where teaching is done on a more relaxed schedule.

Sometimes, different school sessions are designed for different purposes, depending on how extensive a given student wants his training to be or what he can afford. You may find schools offering sessions lasting from one or two weeks for casual or recreational training on up to five or six weeks for more in-depth professional training.

No amount of schooling will ever qualify you as an experienced guide. Only real-world experience can do that. Generally speaking, though, the more time you spend in school, the more you're likely to learn and the better prepared you'll be to start gaining experience out in the real world.

The school I attended ran a full six weeks, with classes and instruction keeping us busy from daylight to dark at least six days a week and usually at least half of the seventh day. Schools lasting shorter lengths of time or offering less intensive instruction may still prepare a student adequately to start out on his first guiding job. However, after getting a first-hand look at the value of lengthy, intensive training, I would recommend choosing the most thorough school you can afford.

Curriculum

It's important to choose a school that follows a specific curriculum. Most well-run schools will include a listing of their curriculum in the brochures and information they send out to prospective students. If not, make sure you get a copy before enrolling. This is crucial for several reasons.

First-off, an outfitter without a well organized plan of action will probably not be organized or professional enough to run a school well or teach thoroughly. He may have good ideas in his head as to what subjects he plans to cover and what schedule he plans to go by. But without a curriculum he may forget to cover certain important details, or

The quality of your training is important. Choose a school that uses only well experienced guides, or better yet outfitters, who can give you thorough instruction.

he may conveniently decide to drop certain important subjects if circumstances don't go as planned.

Secondly, if a school doesn't send out a copy of its curriculum before you enroll, you have no way of holding the staff accountable. When the student sued the guide school in 1990 for not teaching what he was told they would teach, he would have had no grounds without a copy of the curriculum they said they would follow.

Again, with no governing board, anyone can open a guide school and can teach (or neglect to teach) whatever he chooses. Rumors abound that many guide schools simply use students to do the outfitter's haying, camp set-up, etc. under the guise of teaching them what a guide needs to know. Without a copy of the curriculum a guide school promises to teach, you'll have few grounds for legal recourse if you feel the school has failed you.

Thirdly, knowing what a school teaches lets you evaluate and compare. You may decide just by looking at a school's curriculum that it's the one you want to attend. Or you may want to compare several different schools' curriculums and decide which one appears most complete. When choosing a school myself, I picked the one that offered the most, and I have no regrets.

Instructors

Another point to look into when choosing a school is the quality of its instructors. Does it use experienced guides or, better yet, experienced outfitters as teachers? Or does it just use guides who went through the same school last year and now consider themselves experts?

Granted, many of the basics taught in guide schools are simply "head knowledge" and could be taught by someone without a great deal of experience. But in order to be able to teach thoroughly, an instructor must have a wide-enough range of experience to know the extra little tricks of the trade, as well as how and when to apply them. When it comes to just head knowledge, a student can get most of that out of books on his own. If you're paying for "hands-on" resident instruction, insist on well experienced teachers.

Student Evaluation

It would do little good to attend a school from which every student automatically passes. True, you still might learn some things at that school. But you wouldn't learn near as much there as at a school

A school that doesn't grade your work may be doing you few favors. Choose a school where qualified instructors evaluate your performance and expect you to pass minimum standards before sending you out into the real world.

that sets minimum standards for students to achieve and be evaluated by.

The thought of being held to a rigid standard and having to achieve minimum requirements may take some of the glamour and appeal out of attending a guide school. It means putting forth extra effort and self-discipline, both mentally and physically. But if you want the most for your money — if you want a good preparation and learning foundation with which to start guiding — you will be wise to enroll in a school that sets high standards for you and evaluates your learning by those standards.

The school I attended gives a certificate of completion to any student who sticks it out and makes reasonable effort to complete its full course without quitting. That's fine. But it awards diplomas and job placement only to students who achieve fairly rigid and rigorous standards in their learning and performance. I would recommend choosing a school with similar requirements.

Rather than viewing a grading system as something to dread, see it as a set of standards to shoot for and measure your achievement by. True, a grading scale lets the school staff evaluate your qualifications for a guiding job. But more importantly, it lets you evaluate your own progress and achievements and take pride in the work you do.

Placement Service

Unless you have already established a good contact with a reputable outfitter who wants to hire a trained guide, there's little value in attending a school that offers no placement service for graduates. Sure, you might still wrangle up a job for yourself after you've graduated. But it would cost you a lot of phone calls and a lot of time, and you still wouldn't know how reliable a given outfitter is until you showed up to work for him.

Any school that's known for producing well-trained guides will have a waiting list of outfitters looking to hire its graduates. As our society becomes more and more urbanized, experienced guides are harder to come by. More and more outfitters are looking toward schools in order to find guides, and a well-run school will offer placement services for its graduates.

Many outfitters are still leery of school-trained guides, and understandably so. No school can make an experienced guide of anyone, and some don't even do an adequate job of teaching the basics. I've heard of outfitters hiring graduates from some of the poorer schools and then finding that those "guides" still don't even know such simple basics as how to cargo up loads to sling on a pack horse or mule.

Even the best school can only give a basic foundation from which to start gaining real-world experience. However, once an outfitter has had a good experience with a well trained guide-school graduate, he'll usually change his mind. More and more outfitters are seeing the value in hiring guides trained in schools rather than having to spend their own time teaching the basics. That's why a placement service is so valuable to a student.

An outfitter offering a placement service should have a better idea than you do as to which outfitters are reputable, which will pay you the best, and which ones you should avoid. Granted, no outfitter can guarantee the job he places you on will work out perfectly. I know of a few situations where guides were placed with outfitters who turned out to be crooked, or drunks, or otherwise not worth working for. But usually an outfitter who runs his operation well will know where to send you and where not to.

One other point to be careful of is a promise of "guaranteed placement." Under that type of guarantee the student would probably be hired either by the outfitter running the school or by one of his close friends.

No outfitter knows ahead-of-time whether a prospective student has the potential or the ambition and commitment needed to become a qualified guide. An outfitter who would risk having to hire a poorly qualified guide must be willing to run his outfit with that type of crew. Chances are you wouldn't want to work for him.

That's not to say you couldn't get good training at such a school. It's just a warning to look closely before jumping in with both feet. After guiding for several years I once asked an outfitter if he offered that guarantee with the school he ran. His response was, "You've been in this business long enough by now to know I can't make any guarantees!"

If you do enroll in a school that makes such a guarantee, at least find out ahead-of-time what minimum salary would be guaranteed along with the job placement, and where that placement would be.

References

It goes without saying that you should check references before enrolling in a school. Most outfitters will provide them without being asked. The references provided, though, will usually be those who did well in the school and went on to good experiences and successful careers. That's just good business sense.

You might be wise, however, to ask for references who failed to graduate as well. Ask them if they feel the school was well run and if they feel they got a fair shake even though they didn't pass minimum requirements. Remember that such a student may simply be bitter and blame his failure on the school when he really should blame himself. But also keep in mind that if those students didn't pass, there's no guarantee you will either. At least make sure you'll get a fair shot at it.

Parting Shots

In reality, most guide schools probably aren't big money-makers. Most outfitters who run schools seem do it mainly so they can get trained guides themselves — and train those guides the way they want them. They often hire the cream of their own crop.

Remember also that there are no governing boards to regulate guide schools. Consequently the quality of a school depends entirely on the professionalism and commitment of the outfitter running it. Naturally, that means there are good schools being run, but there are also a few bad ones. "Let the buyer beware."

The most positive closing note I can relate would again be my own experience. Before choosing a guide school I wrote to several and compared their curriculums. I noticed that one school offered everything the others did as well as some things the others didn't. I settled on the school that looked most professional and that I thought would give me the most complete training. I found it was booked up for the year.

Another school was offering a substantial discount in order to fill its classes. However, rather than settle for second best I asked to be put on a waiting list in case an unexpected opening came up with my first choice of schools. By Providence, that opening came up, and as a result I enjoyed eight fantastic years in a guiding career. By choosing a school carefully and taking pains to make sure I got into a good one, I got off to the right kind of start.

When you pause on the pass, look over miles of good country, and admire the racks lashed atop your pack string your only regret will probably be that you waited so long to become a guide.

APPENDIX A

STATE OR PROVINCE
OUTFITTER/GUIDE ORGANIZATIONS

For directories or listings of licensed outfitters, contact these professional organizations or state licensing agencies.

IN THE UNITED STATES:

ALASKA

Alaska Professional Hunters Association
P.O. Box 91932
Anchorage, AK 99509
(907) 522-3221 (9 a.m. to 1 p.m. weekdays, Alaska Time Zone)

$5.00 for quarterly listing/publication

-OR-

State of Alaska
Department of Commerce and Economic Development
Division of Occupational Licensing
P.O. Box 110806
Juneau, AK 99811-0806
(907) 465-2572

ARIZONA

Arizona Professional Guides & Outfitters Association
Box 2765
Globe, AZ 85502-2765
(602) 689-2891

-OR-

Information Services
Arizona Game & Fish Department
2221 West Greenway Road
Phoenix, AZ 85023
(602) 942-3000

CALIFORNIA

California Eastern High Sierra Packers Association
Rt. 1, Box 162
Mammoth Lakes, CA 93546
(619) 872-2434 (winter)
(619) 935-4324 (summer)

-OR-

California Department of Fish and Game
License and Revenue Branch
3211 S. Street
Sacramento, CA 95816
(916) 227-2244

COLORADO

Colorado Outfitters Association
P.O. Box 440021
Aurora, CO 80044
(303) 368-4731

-OR-

Colorado Board of Guides & Outfitters
Department of Regulatory Agencies
1560 Broadway, Suite 1340
Denver, CO 80202
(303) 894-7778

IDAHO

Idaho Outfitters and Guides Association
P.O. Box 95
Boise, ID 83701
(208) 342-1919

-OR-

Idaho Outfitters and Guides Licensing Board
1365 N. Orchard, Rm. 172
Boise, ID 83706
(208) 327- 7380

MONTANA

Montana Outfitters and Guides Association
P.O. Box 1248
Helena, MT 59624
(406) 449-3578

-OR-

Board of Outfitters
Department of Commerce
1424 9th Avenue
Helena, MT 59620
(406) 444-3737

NEVADA

Nevada Outfitter & Guide Association
Box 135
Wells, NV 89835
(702) 752-3040

-OR-

Nevada Division of Wildlife
Bureau of Law Enforcement
P.O. Box 10678
Reno, NV 89520-0022
(702) 668-1500

NEW MEXICO

New Mexico Council of Outfitters and Guides
160 Washington S.E., #75
Albuquerque, NM 87108
(505) 743-2502

As of this writing, outfitters and guides in New Mexico are not licensed by any public agency. The New Mexico Council of Outfitters and Guides would be the only likely source for a comprehensive listing of outfitters.

OREGON

Oregon Guides and Packers Association
P.O. Box 10841
Eugene, OR 97440
(503) 683-9552

-OR-

Oregon State Marine Board
435 Commercial St. N.E.
Salem, OR 97310
(503) 373-1405 ext. 225

Oregon's State Marine Board keeps a listing of licensed outfitters strictly for law enforcement purposes. The Board charges $50.00 for that list. However, if a prospective guide wanted to check on an outfitter listed in the Guides and Packers Association directory, the board would verify that particular outfitter's license status.

UTAH

Utah Guides and Outfitters
153 E. 7200 S.
Midvale, UT 84047
(801) 566-2662

-OR-

Utah Division of Wildlife Resources
1596 West North Temple
Salt Lake City, UT 84116-3195
(801) 538-4700

WASHINGTON

Washington Outfitter and Guides Association
22845 N.E. 8th, Suite 331
Redmond, WA 98053
(206) 392-6107

The Washington Department of Wildlife requires a complicated "public disclosure process" in order to release its list of licensed outfitters. The Washington Outfitter and Guides Association would be the only likely source for a comprehensive outfitter listing.

WYOMING

Wyoming Outfitters and Guides Association
P.O. Box 2284
Cody, WY 82414
(307) 527-7453

-OR-

Wyoming Game and Fish Department
Cheyenne, WY 82002
(307) 777-4601

IN CANADA:

ALBERTA

Professional Outfitters Association of Alberta
P.O. Box 67012
Meadowlark Park Postal Office
Edmonton, AB T5R 5Y3
(403) 486-3050

BRITISH COLUMBIA

Guide/Outfitters Association of British Columbia
P.O. Box 759
100 Mile House, B.C. V0K 2E0
(604) 395-2438

NORTHWEST TERRITORIES

Department of Economic Development and Tourism
Government of Northwest Territories
P.O. Box 1320
Yellowknife, NWT X1A 2L9
(800) 661-0788

YUKON TERRITORY

Yukon Outfitters Association
P.O. Box 4548
Whitehorse, Yukon Territory Y1A 2R8
(403) 668-4118

APPENDIX B

NOTE ON GUIDE SCHOOLS AND GUIDE TRAINING

Originally, my intention was to include a complete listing of the guide schools in the various states and provinces. However, that goal proved unrealistic. Because guide schools are not regulated in most states or provinces, few licensing agencies or outfitter associations seem to keep a thorough listing. Tracking them all down would be virtually impossible.

Also, guide schools sometimes come and go, although more seem to be coming than going. With schools in such a state of flux, a list of schools published this year might be badly outdated next year. As outfits change hands, new schools spring up, and a few schools fall by the wayside, that list would soon become obsolete.

A third consideration is that not all guide schools are run well enough nor have some developed an adequate curriculum to be recommended. Without attending each one, I would have no way of sorting out which schools are worth a student's time and money, and which should be avoided. Although my proposed listing would not have endorsed any particular school, there's always the risk of inadvertently steering students toward a bad one.

In the end, maybe its best that students search out the possibilities on their own. That way, the more serious schools and the more serious students will more likely find each other. The schools less professionally run, and students less diligent in their school search will less likely get crossed up and run into trouble. That's probably best in the long run.

ADDITIONAL GUIDE TRAINING

Those already in the guiding profession often find a need for more extensive training, particularly regarding natural history interpretation. They find that a more thorough knowledge of the wild plants, animals and other resources they deal with would better enable them to provide a well rounded experience for their clients. The following organizations provide that type of interpretive training:

THE PROFESSIONAL GUIDE INSTITUTE

As one outfitter recently stated, "The outfitting industry recognizes a need for better trained guides." The Professional Guide Institute was created in order to meet that need. In the spring of 1991 a number of outfitters and land-use agency officials began designing a training curriculum for guides. Its intent is to increase professionalism in the outfitting industry by enhancing guides' knowledge of the resources they deal with as well as their ability to share that knowledge.

The Professional Guide Institute (PGI) is not designed to train people how to be guides. Its steering committee believes that experience is still the best teacher. Rather, the Institute's curriculum is "auxiliary to experience." As Dr. Richard Clark, one of PGI's founders and leaders says, "It will help make you a good guide, but it won't make you *a* guide."

At this point PGI offers four different programs: Wildlands Heritage, Backcountry Leadership, Wildlands Interpretation, and Outfitter Operations. By 1996 the Institute plans to begin offering its courses throughout the northern Rocky Mountain region and even nationally. Plans may also include correspondence courses.

For more information contact:

Professional Guide Institute
Attn. Grant Simonds
P.O. Box 95
Boise, ID 83701
(208) 342-1438

Canyonlands Field Institute
P.O. Box 68
Moab, UT 84532
(801) 259-7750

Yellowstone Institute
P.O. Box 117
Yellowstone National Park, WY 82190
(307) 344-2294

APPENDIX C

RECOMMENDED READING/VIEWING

Back, Joe
     Horses, Hitches and Rocky Trails
      "The Packer's Bible"
     Johnson Books
     Boulder, CO 1959

Back, Joe and Vic Lemmon
     The Old Guide Remembers, The Young Guide
     Finds Out
     Johnson Books
     Boulder, CO 1986

Brown, Bill and Smoke Elser
     Packin' In On Mules and Horses
     Mountain Press Publishing Co.
     Missoula, MT 1980

Burk, Dale
     Camp Cookbook
     Stoneydale Press
     Stevensville, MT 1993

Cheff, Bud
     Indian Trails and Grizzly Tales
     Stoneydale Press
     Stevensville, MT 1993

Copenhaver, Howard
     They Left Their Tracks
     Stoneydale Press
     Stevensville, MT 1990

Copenhaver, Howard

More Tracks
Stoneydale Press
Stevensville, MT 1992

Russell, Andy

Grizzly Country
Alfred A. Knopf
New York, NY 1967

Russell, Andy

Horns in the High Country
Alfred A. Knopf
New York, NY 1973

Russell, Andy

Trails of a Wilderness Wanderer
Alfred A. Knopf
New York, NY 1971

Sager, Bill and Duncan Gilchrist

Field Care Handbook
Stoneydale Press
Stevensville, MT 1995

Van Zwoll, Wayne

Elk Rifles, Cartridges and Hunting Tactics
Wayne Van Zwoll
Bridgeport, WA 1992

Young, Ralph W.

Grizzlies Don't Come Easy: My Life as an Alaskan Bear Hunter
Winchester Press, Tulsa 1981

Video:

Ghost Riders Leave No Trace
Banff National Park
Box 900, Banff, AB, Canada
T0L 0C0

LISTING OF BOOKS

Additional copies of SO YOU REALLY WANT TO BE A GUIDE, and many other of Stoneydale Press' books on outdoor recreation, big game hunting, or historical reminisces centered around the Northern Rocky Mountain region, are available at many book stores and sporting goods stores, or direct from Stoneydale Press. If you'd like more information, or like to make an order, you can contact us by calling a toll free number, 1-800-735-7006, or writing the address at the bottom of the next page. Here's a partial listing of some of the books that are available:

Cookbooks

Camp Cookbook, Featuring Recipes for Fixing Both at Home and in Camp, With Field Stories by Dale A. Burk, 216 pages, comb binding

Cooking for Your Hunter, By Miriam Jones, 180 pages, comb binding

Historical Reminisces

Hunting Adventures Worldwide, By Jack Atcheson. Collection of wonderful reminisces by one of hunting's greatest figures. Big 256 pages, 80 photographs, hardcover only.

Indian Trails & Grizzly Tales, By Bud Cheff Sr., 212 pages, available in clothbound and softcover editions.

They Left Their Tracks, By Howard Copenhaver, Recollections of Sixty Years as a Wilderness Outfitter, 192 pages, clothbound or softcover editions (One of our all-time most popular books.)

More Tracks, By Howard Copenhaver, 78 Years of Mountains, People & Happiness, 180 pages, clothbound or softcover editions

Mules & Mountains, By Margie E. Hahn, the story of Walt Hahn, Forest Service Packer, 164 pages, clothbound or softcover editions

Hunting Books

Bugling for Elk, By Dwight Schuh, the bible on hunting early-season elk. A recognized classic, 164 pages, softcover edition only.

Coyote Hunting, By Phil Simonski. Presents basics on hunting coyotes as well as caring for the pelts, 126 pages, many photographs, softcover only.

Elk Hunting in the Northern Rockies, By Ed Wolff. Uses expertise of five recognized elk hunting experts to show the five basic concepts used to hunt elk. Another of our very popular books, 162 pages, many photographs.

Field Care Handbook For The Hunter & Fisherman, By Bill Sager & Duncan Gilchrist, 168 pages, comb binding, many photographs and illustrations. The most comprehensive field care handbook available.

Hunting Open Country Mule Deer, By Dwight Schuh. Simply the best and most detailed book ever done for getting in close to big mule deer. The ultimate mule deer book by a recognized master, 14 chapters, 180 pages.

Montana Hunting Guide, By Dale A. Burk, the most comprehensive and fact-filled guidebook available on hunting in Montana, 192 pages, clothbound or softcover editions.

Taking Big Bucks, By Ed Wolff. Subtitled "Solving the Whitetail Riddle," this book presents advice from top whitetail experts with an emphasis on hunting western whitetails. 176 pages, 62 photographs.

Radical Elk Hunting Strategies, By Mike Lapinski. Takes over where other books on early-season elk hunting leave off to give advice on what the hunter must do to adapt to changing conditions. 162 pages, 70 photographs.

Western Hunting Guide, By Mike Lapinski, the most thorough guide on hunting the western states available. A listing of where-to-go in the western states alone makes the book a valuable reference tool, 168 pages, clothbound or softcover editions.

STONEYDALE PRESS PUBLISHING COMPANY
523 Main Street • Drawer B
Stevensville, Montana 59870
Phone: 406-777-2729